Shakespeare's THE MERCHANT OF VENICE

LAURA LIPPMAN
DEPARTMENT OF ENGLISH
HARVARD UNIVERSITY

MONARCH PRESS

Published by
MONARCH PRESS
a division of Simon & Schuster, Inc.
1 West 39th Street
New York, N.Y. 10018

Standard Book Number: 671-00637-1

Library of Congress Catalog Card Number: 65-7228

Printed in the United States of America

TABLE OF CONTENTS

INTRODUCTION

Life of Shakespeare

William Shakespeare was born in Stratford-on-Avon in April, 1564. He was the third of eight children (the oldest of the four who survived) born to John and Mary Shakespeare. John Shakespeare was a successful merchant who, after holding various minor muncipal positions, was elected Bailiff (Mayor) of Stratford in 1568. As the son of a prominent family, William doubtless attended the town grammar school, which prepared the sons of the local burghers for entry to a university. This was the only formal schooling that he ever had, and here he must have learned the "small Latin and less Greek" with which his friend the poet Ben Jonson credited him.

In 1582 at the age of eighteen, Shakespeare married Anne Hathaway, eight years his senior, and six months later their daughter Susanna was born. It has been argued that the marriage was forced because Anne was already pregnant, but this does not necessarily follow. Betrothal was considered legally binding, and conjugal rights were often performed before the wedding took place. In any case, the marriage does not seem to have been a very happy one. In 1585 twins were born to the couple, a boy and a girl, named Hamnet and Judith. By this year John Shakespeare was in less comfortable financial circumstances, and about the same time William Shakespeare left Stratford to seek his fortune, leaving his family behind.

No records remain to tell us what Shakespeare did in the years of his early twenties, although tradition has it that he spent part of the time as a country schoolmaster. It is certain, however, that during this time he became an actor and playwright. The poet Robert Breene, in his *Groatsworth of Wit* (1592), railed against "an upstart crow beautified with our feathers, that with his Tiger's heart wrapt in a player's hide supposes he is as well able to bombast out a blank verse as the best of you. . . . in his own conceit the only Shake-scene in a country." The reference to a tiger's skin is a parody of a line in *Henry VI*, and Shake-scene, of course, is a broad hint at Shakespeare. Probably in 1593 and 1594, while the London theaters were closed by the plague, Shakespeare wrote two narrative poems, *Venus and Adonis* and *the Rape of Lucrece*, dedicated to the Earl of Southamptom. He also wrote the famous sonnets, probably during the 1590's, which were published in 1609 without his consent.

Before 1594 Shakespeare became a member of a theater repertory company called The Chamberlain's Men (later changed to The King's Men). He remained with his company for the rest of his career, serving in the capacity of actor as well as playwright. Outstanding among the other members were Richard Burbage (generally playing the serious lead role), Will Kempe (the clown), and Edward Alleyn (the original Shylock). The Lord Chamberlain's Men performed in various theaters in London and the surrounding countryside until its own theater, the Globe, was built in 1599, some years after *The Merchant of Venice* was first produced.

Shakespeare's earliest plays, written before 1594, are rather conventional works of comedy, melodrama, and history (including *Comedy of Errors, Titus Andronicus,* and *Henry VI).* By 1594 his plays more clearly show the stature of his genius. Among these plays of his early middle years are the comedies *A Midsummer Night's Dream* and *The Merchant of Venice;* the tragedy *Romeo and Juliet;* and the histories, Richard II, *Henry IV* in two parts, and *Henry V.*

During the period from 1599 to 1606, he wrote the great tragedies, *Hamlet, Othello, King Lear,* and *Macbeth.* Concurrently, he wrote the "dark" or "problem" comedies, *All's Well that Ends Well, Troilus and Cressida,* and *Measure for Measure.* Finally, between 1608 and 1611, he wrote the romantic comedies, *Cymbeline, The Winter's Tale,* and *The Tempest.*

While Shakespeare lived in London his family remained in Stratford. In 1596 his son Hamnet died, and in 1607 and 1616 his daughters married. Shakespeare was the most popular playwright of his day, and with success came the money with which he bought his father a coat of arms (enabling him to become a gentleman). For himself, he bought New Place, one of the most elegant houses in Stratford. In 1611, when he retired from London, Shakespeare returned to live in New Place, where he died in April, 1616. He was buried in Stratford's Trinity Church and a monument was shortly thereafter erected to his memory.

HISTORICAL BACKGROUND OF THE MERCHANT OF VENICE. The characterization of Shylock, the Jewish moneylender of Venice, has attracted more than a fair share of the critical interest in the play. Like Falstaff in Shakespeare's history plays, Shylock has become one of the immortal characters in English literature, upstaging the titular hero of his play and casting grave doubts on Shakespeare's intentions and apparent anti-Semitism. Historical scholars and critics of our time have made two things clear, that Shakespeare intended the noble Antonio as the hero of the play and that Shakespeare was not actively engaged in an anti-Semitic crusade.

From the earliest years of the English Renaissance in the sixteenth century, English philosophers and scholars looked to Italy, where the body of humanist learning was evolving in the neo-Platonic Christian schools. Emerging from the Middle Ages, which early humanists regarded as a crude and barbarous period, they searched for a pattern of gentility by which they could cultivate and civilize the rude manners and language of their age. Books like Ascham's *Scholemaster,* Elyot's *Boke of the Governour,* Lyly's *Euphues,* Sidney's *Arcadia,* and Spenser's *Faerie Queene* proposed systems of behavior and standards of morality which the educated gentleman and courtier was expected to follow. The ideals of the perfect Christian gentleman, which had been formulated in Italy, were most completely expressed in Baldassare Castiglione's *Il Cortegiano* (*The Book of the Courtier*), written in 1508 and published in Italy in 1528. This book, subsequently translated into English by Thomas Hoby and published in 1561 and 1588, had a wide influence on English thought, manners, and literature, and is probably the best source book for understanding the characterization of Shakespeare's heroes. The young Prince Hal (hero of two of Shakespeare's history plays) was used as an illustration in Elyot's book on the education of a prince, who was expected to be profligate in youth but well-tempered and wise in maturity. Hal is so developed in the two parts of *Henry IV*, and in *Henry V*, that he is the ideal prince. Hamlet also displays all the marks of the perfect courtier, soldier, scholar, friend, and lover, which combined to make the ideal Renaissance gentleman. The same system of thought must be applied to Antonio and Bassanio, two gentlemen in *The Merchant of Venice*. Antonio, the titular and actual hero of the play, is an older man who has achieved the sobriety of maturity. Bassanio is just emerging from the prodigal ways of youth. Together they display the realized and potential gentility of the perfect Renaissance man. Shakespeare wrote *The Merchant of Venice* as a romantic comedy, in which the heroic Antonio serves as a model for all good men and through whose passionate friendship and Christian generosity Bassanio, Lorenzo, and Shylock are led to the good way of life.

Fortunately or unfortunately, Shakespeare's powers of characterization were far too rich to enable him to subordinate the fascinating and repulsive personality of Shylock to his sober and humble hero. The critic Charlee Norton Coe perceptively notes that Shylock is "overcharacterized" for the role he was intended to play; that Shakespeare had become too interested in the role he was creating to effect a favorable balance between the comic subordinating player, Shylock, and the intended hero of the play, Antonio. More than a century of sentimental Romantic criticism has helped to increase misunderstandings about the play by concentrating on the humanitarian justification of Shylock as the victim of Christian intolerance. A proper balance can be restored to the reading of *The Merchant* when it is understood that Shakespeare knew and was interested in the Elizabethan gentleman, that he purchased a coat of arms and the right to be called gentleman for his father and himself, and that he himself displayed the virtues and ideals of the perfect Renaissance man.

The research of J. L. Cardozo in *The Contemporary Jew in Elizabethan Drama* has made it clear that Shakespeare did not know any Jews personally and that he was not actively engaged in an anti-Semitic crusade. He was simply following a centuries-old stereotype of the Jewish people which had penetrated the life and literature of western Europe and survived in England long after the Jews had been exiled from that country. It is to Shakespeare's credit that he was able to impart human qualities to Shylock even while he perpetuated the stereotype; he created a living portrait that has caused critics to wonder whether Shylock is merely a comic villain or the tragic victim of Christian cruelty.

The story of the Jews in medieval Europe throws a good deal of light on the events of the play and provides us with the Shakespearean frame of reference which is necessary for an understanding of both the major themes and minor details which are the fabric of *The Merchant of Venice*. During the entire Middle Ages, the Jewish people were alternately protected and persecuted by the temporal powers of whatever land they inhabited. Their experience in England is typical of their history in Christianized Europe. After the Norman Conquest in 1066, Jewish people, fleeing from the persecutions of the French clergy, made their way to England. Economic possibilities were offered in the newly conquered country, and the Normans wanted the tribute money and the financial experience for making business transactions, which only the Jews could provide. It had been established by the Church long before that Christians were not to lend money at interest, for to do so would be a violation of the *New Testament* concept of charity. Restricted as they were from owning real property and keeping serfs, which were essential to the agrarian economy of the Middle Ages, more and more Jews became tradesmen and financiers. Although they were generally abused because of their religious differences, Jews were also frequently tolerated and invited into a country to stabilize its shaky financial structure.

During the two centuries following the Conquest, Jews continued to emigrate to England, usually in order to escape from overzealous crusaders. A liberal charter was granted them by Henry I (1100-35) in exchange for a percentage of their profits in all trade and moneylending transactions. The King became the heir of every Jew and took over his estate upon death. Consequently, moneylenders were forced to charge high interest rates, which increased as the King's demands grew. Thus, the Jew became the buffer for the King's extortions and the symbol of the hated usurer. He was, in effect, the King's scapegoat.

Religious persecution was added to the economic pressures on the Jews in England after Aquitaine became part of England's domain. At the coronation of Richard I (the Lion-hearted), systematic massacres and immolations of Jews formed part of the people's coronation celebrations. By the end of the twelfth century, legal spoilation and extortion of the Jews in England matched that on the continent, only more openly. Richard, for example, required the registration of all Jewish moneylending businesses and had state records kept of all lending transactions. To this end, he herded all Jews into the larger cities where records were being kept. John Lackland, Richard's brother and successor, replenished some of his depleted funds by imprisoning or executing Jews on various charges in order to seize their properties. At the same time, he gave them protection in the city of Lincoln, where he established the Jews as the King's chattel (property, livestock), making it illegal for anyone to injure the King's Jews just as it was illegal to harm the King's hounds. (The Jew and the dog will be associated frequently in *The Merchant of Venice*.)

By 1254, conditions were so bad that the Jewish people petitioned the King to allow them to leave the country. After some delay, they were finally ordered out by Edward I. By October of 1290, sixteen thousand

Jews had left the country, sailing to Flanders, Germany, and Spain where they were alternately tolerated for their financial prowess, persecuted for their religious "stubbornness," and forced into conversion, slavery, and suicide. England did not see Jews again until the latter half of the seventeenth century, when the Puritan protector Cromwell allowed them to return.

It can be seen from Shakespeare's treatment of Shylock, from the allusions Shylock makes to the persecutions and humiliations suffered at the hands of Christians, that Shakespeare was familiar with the plight of the Jewish people in the Christian world, that he created an appropriate and accurate background for the character of Shylock, and that he did not find Antonio's abuse of Shylock inconsistent with the character of the perfect Renaissance gentleman. In fact, the final forced conversion of Shylock, from the Renaissance Christian point of view, was regarded as a kindness to the obstinate Jew, who had stubbornly refused, through the centuries, to accept Christ as the Messiah, to adopt the Christian faith, and thereby secure salvation in heaven, which Christ promised only to his followers. With Christ's life as an example, the only Christian thing to do was to follow the Gospel's precepts and convert the Jews.

THE LITERARY BACKGROUND. During the Jews' four-hundred year absence from England, legends from the continent helped to perpetuate English stereotypes of the Jews. It had become conventional in Europe to attribute unexplained deaths, plagues, and other disasters to Jewish hatred for Christians and their desire for revenge against their persecutors.

Jews and devils were thought of as alter-egos, and stories of ritual murders and poisoned wells grew into an extensive literature. In the Old English poem, *Elene*, written long before the Jews came to England, Jews were accused of concealing the true cross; Chaucer's tale of the Prioress charged a Jew with the murder of a nameless little boy because of his devotion to the Virgin, and the miracle plays of the late Middle Ages portrayed *Old Testament* figures as wicked and comic characters.

By Shakespeare's boyhood, the character of Judas Iscariot was conventionalized as the embodiment of all that was evil. Judas had evolved as a low-comic character, usually portrayed by an actor in a red wig, red beard, and long nose (as Shylock was played until well into the eighteenth century). The Judas would become the victim of playful beatings by other characters in the play, and members of the audience were allow-to use him as a scapegoat.

In Tudor England, the Jew was purely a dramatic or literary figure, for there were few known Jews living in the country at the time. It is true, however, that the 1594 trial of Dr. Roderigo Lopez, a Portuguese Christian convert and physician to Queen Elizabeth who was accused of an attempt on her life, may have suggested the idea for Shakespeare's Shylock. But Lopez was already a convert and was involved in a plot which did not involve his Jewish heritage. Shylock is too much like the conventional Jew of English literature to resemble Lopez. Even so, considerable interest was aroused by the trial of Lopez, and the historical scholar John Palmer insists that anti-Semitism was in fashion "when Shakespeare sat down to write 'The Merchant of Venice.'" E. E. Stoll adds that Marlowe's play, *The Jew of Malta* (c. 1588), remained popular over a period of four years, and during the trial of Lopez between May and December, 1594, the play was performed twenty times. Marlowe's play featured the Jew Barabas who embodied "all the qualities which a persecuting majority commonly attributed to its victims" and demonstrated that, in the theater, anti-Semitism was the popular view. Barabas in Marlowe's play is abused by the governor of Malta. Along with other rich Jews, he is required to give half his estate to pay tribute to the Turks. When Barabas refuses, he is deprived of his entire estate. From then on, he becomes the personification of evil and a statement of the essential greed, cruelty, ambition, and treachery of the stereotyped Jew. Partly out of revenge, partly out of his hatred for Christians, Barabas helps the Turks take Malta, then assists the governor of Malta in a counterplot against the Turks, which he fails of achieving because he accidentally falls into the boiling cauldron he has prepared for the Turks.

Shakespeare's Shylock has the same motives as Barabas. He admits his hatred of Christians in general and on one Christian in particular, Antonio, because of their ill-treatment of Shylock's people and his own person. Like Barabas, Shylock is moved by the desire for general and particular revenge. However, he is not merely a conventional stage Jew or symbol of evil and hatred; Shylock is endowed with human quualities and is given specific motives for revenge. He has been spat upon, called dog, vilified for pursuing the only trade which the Christian world has left open to him; he has had his daughter "stolen" by a Christian, and for this he is expected to show mercy. As the conventional Jew, he remains staunch in his cruelty, just as Antonio, the epitome of Christian love, humility, charity, friendship, and forgiveness, willingly accepts his fate at the hands of his enemy. Antonio shows true Christian spirit in his submission to the injuries he must endure even to the point of death, while Shylock, like the vengeful God of the *Old Testament*, demands that the letter of the law be carried out.

SOURCES OF *THE MERCHANT OF VENICE*. The two intertwining stories of the play were familiar to Shakespeare from the existing body of European literature. Tales about usurers were fairly common, and the theme of the pound-of-flesh has ancient analogues in religious tales of Persia and India. It appeared in various western versions, particularly in Italian sources In at least one of these the Jew is not the villain but the victim of the contract. Leti's *Viat di Sisto Quinta* tells of a Christian merchant who (in 1585) wins a wager from a Jew and claims his pound of flesh according to the bargain, before the Pope intervenes to save the unfortunate Jew. An English variant, Anthony Munday's *Zelauto* (1580), tells of two university students who, with their wives, outwit their creditor's demand for his pound of flesh, and in this case all participants are Christian. It has been suggested by some scholars that a lost play called *The Jew* was actually Shakespeare's main source for *The Merchant of Venice,* for it was described by Gosson in 1579 as "representing the greediness of worldly chusers, and bloody mindes of Usurers." However, since the text of this play is lost, it is impossible to determine to what extent Shakespeare drew upon it.

The Merchant of Venice does, however, bear very strong resemblance to a tale in the Italian collection, *Il Pecorone,* which had been compiled in 1378 by Ser Giovanni Fiorentino but was not published until 1558. The story tells of a young man, Gianetto, who woos and finally wins the Lady of Belmont, aided financially by his godfather Ansaldo. The Lady of Belmont has agreed to marry any man who can manage to stay awake in bed with her long enough to take advantage of his situation. Many men have tried and all have failed because of a sleeping potion that the Lady secretly slips them before they retire to bed. After two unsuccessful attempts, Gianetto learns from the Lady's maid the secret of the drugged nightcap, and the next time he only pretends to drink it. Then, when he is in bed with her, he makes the most of his wakefulness and the Lady agrees to marry him. In the meantime, however, his godfather is in trouble. In order to finance Gianetto's three voyages to Belmont, Ansaldo had borrowed money from a Jew to whom he had promised to pay a pound of flesh if the money was forfeit. Just as in Shakespeare's play, this potential victim is saved by the Lady who, disguised as a lawyer, defends him in court. The final confusion over the ring is also included in this tale, which ends in happiness for all except the Jew.

The major change that Shakespeare made in Ser Giovanni's story concerns the lovers. Whereas the Lady of Belmont in the early tale resembles the enchantresses of ancient lore who bewitch their wooers and cruelly mock them, Shakespeare's Portia is a charming, intelligent, and honorable young woman. Her suitors woo her in an entirely different way, one suggested in the compilation of medieval Latin stories, the *Gesta Romanorum* (translated and printed in 1577 and 1595), which includes an account of a young man who must win his lady by choosing among three caskets. This device is theatrically more effective than the bedroom plot, and it also makes the Lady a more virtuous figure than she is in Ser Giovanni.

Thus we see that the main elements of *The Merchant of Venice* are to be found in earlier sources: the usurious Jew, the pound-of-flesh contract, and the wooer who must choose among three caskets. What is so extraordinary about this play, however, is the way in which Shakespeare manages to combine the various themes into a tightly unified and highly poetic whole. The characters of Bassanio, Antonio, Jessica, Lorenzo, Gratiano, and particularly Portia and Shylock, are far more interesting and complex than their predecessors.

DATE AND TEXT. *The Merchant of Venice,* written some time between 1594 and 1598, was first published in 1600 in a good edition called the Heyes Quarto, from which the Quarto of 1619 and the Folio version of 1623 were taken. The Quarto of 1653 provide the first list of characters, which has since been expanded and is now a standard in all texts. The Folio text divided the play into acts and gave a few stage directions, but many stage directions and the scene divisions were provided by later editors.

BRIEF SUMMARY OF THE MERCHANT OF VENICE

Bassanio, a young Venetian nobleman, seeks to win back his fortune and to gain the woman of his heart at one and the same time by marrying Portia of Belmont. He asks his friend the merchant Antonio to lend him the money necessary for the voyage to Belmont. Antonio does not have the cash on hand because his money is tied up at present in ships trading on the seas. However, he gladly uses his credit to borrow the money from Shylock, a Jew and a professional usurer. Shylock is very bitter against Antonio, who has often criticized him for the kind of business he does, but in this case he says he wants to make friends with the Christians. He therefore proposes as a "merry sport" that he will lend the 3,000 ducats for three months and that Antonio will sign a contract, providing that, if the money is not repaid in time, he will forfeit a pound of flesh. Antonio, confident that his ships will return a month before the date, agrees to these terms.

In the meantime, Portia is being wooed by numerous suitors attracted by her wealth, beauty, and virtue. She does not take a fancy to any of them, but she is not free to decide whom she will marry. Her father had stipulated before his death that she must marry whatever man correctly chooses which of three caskets (one gold, one silver, and one lead) contains her picture. Before choosing, her suitors must promise that if they fail to guess correctly, they will never seek to marry at all. This condition frightens away some aspirants, but before Bassanio arrives the Prince of Morroco has already wrongly chosen the gold and the Prince of Arragon the silver casket.

Back in Venice, Bassanio's friend Lorenzo, who is in love with Shylock's daughter Jessica, elopes with the girl, who takes a large part of her father's possessions. Jessica becomes a Christian as well as Lorenzo's wife. Shylock, furious that his daughter has adandoned him, and especially that she has taken so much money and such valuable jewels, feels that the entire Christian community has conspired against him. Meanwhile, he is still anxious to get even with Antonio by claiming the pound of flesh if he is not repaid on time.

Bassanio stays in Belmont for quite some time before finally choosing among the caskets. Portia fervently hopes that he will choose correctly, and he does so, by selecting the lead casket. When Portia and Bassanio marry, Portia's maid, Nerissa, and Bassanio's friend Gratiano (who has accompanied him to Belmont from Venice) also wed. The two women each give their husbands a ring, from which, they tell them, they must never part. Immediately after the betrothal Lorenzo and Jessica arrive, accompanied by Salario, another friend from Venice, who brings Bassanio a letter from Antonio. It seems that Antonio's ships failed to return on time and that his bond to Shylock is forfeit. Although various friends have offered to pay what Antonio owes, Shylock insists on claiming his pound of flesh. Antonio writes that he is prepared to die and only hopes to see his good friend Bassanio once more in life. Appalled by this development, Bassanio (joined by Gratiano) immediately returns to Venice, supplied by his generous wife with three times the sum necessary to repay Shylock.

Portia tells Lorenzo that she and Nerissa will retire to a convent while their husbands are away, and she asks him to remain with Jessica as master and mistress of her estate while she is gone. Actually, Portia and Nerissa set out for Venice, where Portia, disguised as a young lawyer, undertakes the defense of Antonio in court. Shylock demands his pound of flesh and the Duke of Venice, presiding at the trial, reluctantly agrees that his claim must be granted if contracts are to be considered legally binding in Venice. Portia, however, sees a way out of this predicament. First she urges Shylock to be merciful, but when he remains adamant, she says that he may take just one pound of flesh, neither more nor less, and not a drop of blood, for the contract says nothing about blood. If he fails by even a hair's breath of the exact weight, he will be held guilty of breaking the contract. Shylock then agrees to take the original 3,000 ducats, but Portia is not yet finished with him. She says that he is guilty of planning the murder of a Venetian citizen, for which he has incurred the death penalty. This sentence, however, is commuted by the Duke, who tells Shylock that he must convert to Christianity and divide his wealth between Antonio and the state. When Shylock protests that the sentence is too harsh (for he cannot live without any money), Antonio agrees not to claim his full share, provided that Shylock will leave that money to his daughter when he dies. This arrangement concludes the trial scene. Bassanio, anxious to reward the lawyer, offers him a large fee, but the lawyer wants only one thing, the ring on Bassanio's finger. When Antonio urges his friend to give it up, Bassanio reluctantly agrees. At the same time Nerissa, as the lawyer's page, asks for and also gets Gratiano's ring.

In Belmont, meantime, Jessica and Lorenzo pass the time in lyrical happiness together. Launcelot, a clownish character who had been Shylock's servant and is now in Bassanio's service, is delightfully nonsensical in their company.

Portia and Nerissa return home and are followed shortly by Bassanio, Gratiano, and Antonio. Portia welcomes Antonio warmly but, noticing that Bassanio no longer has the ring she gave him, she upbraids him for his faithlessness, while Nerissa does likewise to Gratiano. The two men explain the circumstances in which they parted from the rings; and, after teasing their husbands for a while, the two women confess that they were the lawyer and the page of the court at Venice. On this note of happy surprise the play ends with general joy on all sides.

DETAILED SUMMARY OF *THE MERCHANT OF VENICE*

Act One, Scene One

The scene is a street in Venice. Antonio, a prominent merchant, is talking with his friends Salarino and Salanio. He tells them that he does not know why he is so sad nowadays, and that his sadness wearies him as much as it wearies them.

> **COMMENT:** Antonio is the merchant of the title of the play. The state of depression or "want-wit sadness" which Antonio describes marks him as once as a typical pensive Renaissance man. His show of world-weariness is an inner condition brought about by the idealistic, spiritual, noble nature of the man himself; he has less use for the material realities of the world than for idealistic values he lives by. Antonio's depression is symptomatic of the melancholy man, one whose "humours" or bodily fluids consisted of a preponderance of black choler or black bile. In Medieval and Renaissance physiology, the body was believed to contain four chief fluids: blood, phlegm, choler, and black choler. A predominance of one of these fluids was believed to affect the mental disposition and consequently the behavior of the man. The behavioral characteristics of the melancholy man were, in addition to an unaccountable gloom (such as Hamlet also displays), sullenness and irascibility. It will be seen shortly that Antonio manifests all these symptoms of the melancholy man. He is taciturn of speech and sullen among his friends; and that he is hot-tempered we may guess from his past treatment of Shylock.

Antonio's companions think that he must be worried about business, since he has several ships out on the ocean where anything might happen to them. Salanio tells Antonio, "Believe me, sir, had I such venture forth,/ The better part of my affections would / Be with my hopes abroad." He says that he would be constantly plucking the grass to test the wind's direction, and peering into maps to chart the routes of his vessels. Salarino pursues this train of thought, declaring that he, for his part, would connect every part of his experience with the thought of possible dangers to his ships. Thus, his breath cooling his broth would make him worry about storms at sea; sand running through an hour glass would remind him that ships can founder on dangerous sandbars; and the stone walls of a church would make him think of the treacherous rocks in the sea.

> **COMMENT:** In some editions, Salarino and Salanio are called Salerio and Solanio. Early quartos and folios of the play used various similar abbreviations to designate these characters, and some modern editors attempt to clear up the confusion in names by adopting new forms for them.
>
> Salarino describes the process of associating ideas, a tendency frequently found in Shakespeare himself by Caroline Spurgeon in

Shakespeare's Imagery. Shakespeare repeatedly called up whole groups or chains of ideas by a single word or idea which acted as an emotional or mental stimulus. The meaning of an idea-chain is sometimes clearer in one context than in another and can be used to throw light on some of the obscure passages in Shakespeare. The character's emotional persuasions are often revealed by the explication of an idea-chain, as shall be seen.

Antonio denies that he is melancholy because of business. Not all his fortune is invested at one time and, moreover all his capital is not entrusted in a single ship. It is hardly likely that several vessels will come to a bad end simultaneously. Salanio declares that if is not business it must be love that troubles Antonio, but the merchant denies any romantic attachment. With this explanation ruled out, Salanio falls back on the inexplicable ways of Nature, who has made some strange fellows in her time. The best he can say is that Antonio is sad because he is not merry, which, of course, is not to say anything at all.

COMMENT: Salarino and Salanio speak in rich poetry that evokes the wealth and splendor of Venice. Salarino refers to Antonio's ships as "argosies with portly sail," and compares them to the Venetians he knows, "signiors and rich burghers." Their stately sails tower above their petty competitors, past whom they fly "with woven wings." Antonio's ships are engaged in trade with the exotic Orient, and therefore, when Salarino thinks of a shipwreck he naturally thinks of the loss of precious spices and silks. All in all, Venice seems to be a marvelously glamorous world, where familiarity with the beautiful and the exotic breeds a general gaiety and elegance. Antonio's melancholy puts him at one remove from this Venetian world, but we will see in the rest of the scene how he makes up in nobility of soul for want of sprightliness.

Three more gentlemen enter, Bassanio, Lorenzo, and Gratiano. Salarino and Salanio leave the newcomers to cheer up Antonio if they can, but before they depart they assure Bassanio that they will be delighted to make merry in his company whenever he is available. When they have gone, Gratiano remarks that Antonio is not looking well, and chides the merchant for worrying too much about worldly matters. Antonio denies this charge, declaring, "I hold the world but as the world, Gratiano / A stage where every man must play a part, / And mine a sad one." Gratiano replies that he, for his part, prefers to play the role of the fool, always gay and laughing. He says that he would rather have his liver heated with wine than his heart cold as the marble on a tomb. (Sixteenth-century psychology held that the liver as well as the heart played a part in emotional life.) From this remark about his own predisposition, Gratiano goes on to criticize those men who keep up an appearance of gravity and silence in order to impress the world with their profundity, as if he thought that Antonio were only pretending to be melancholy.

Lorenzo declares that by associating with the loquacious Gratiano he is afraid he will gain the reputation of the kind of false wise man of whom

Gratiano was speaking, for he can never get a word in edgewise as long as Gratiano is around. While Gratiano accepts this rebuke with good humor, Antonio promises to make an effort to talk more. The comical Gratiano is happy to hear this, declaring that silence is only commendable in a dried ox's tail and in an unmarriageable girl.

Lorenzo and Gratiano depart, promising to meet Bassanio for supper. When they have gone, Bassanio declares that "Gratiano speaks an infinite deal of nothing, more than any man in all Venice." His reasons are as obscure as two grains of wheat hid in two bushels of chaff, and worth just as little.

> **COMMENT:** Antonio's explanation that he holds "the world but as the world" is another key to his character. The Renaissance gentleman was schooled in neo-Platonic ideas and adopted the position that the world was only a testing place for the soul of man. Far more important than the world of reality or the material world was the world of the spirit to which the pure soul aspired during its sojourn on earth and to which the soul departed after death. Antonio's promise to talk more in the future reveals another of his aspects as a melancholy man, one who is sullen among his friends.
>
> Gratiano, a fool, is offered as a contrast to the grave and silent wise man whom Antonio represents. That Bassanio recognizes Gratiano's absurdity and still remains his friend is a sign of the former's noble spirit. Associations of this kind were thought to be commendable because the gentleman could instruct the fool on how to mend his ways. By setting a good example, Bassanio does just this for Gratiano.

Antonio asks Bassanio to tell him now, as he promised he would, about that lady "To whom you swore a secret pilgrimage." Instead of answering directly, Bassanio talks about the state of his own finances. He reminds Antonio that because he squandered his fortune and lived beyond his means in his youth, he is now heavily in debt, and chiefly to Antonio, his friend and kinsman. Bassanio is deeply distressed at being unable to repay this debt, but now he has an idea of how to win a new fortune. Antonio begs to know how he may be of service to Bassanio and assures him that "My purse, my person, my extremest means / Lie all unlocked to your occasions."

> **COMMENT:** Antonio in this play represents the principle of noble friendship. His offer to Bassanio of his purse, person, and means is the first of a line of acts which mark him as the ideal friend, one who is willing to set aside his Christian scruples to negotiate a loan for his friend, and who is even willing to die in supporting the cause of his friend.
>
> The Renaissance ideal of the perfect friend developed first in the neo-Platonic schools of Italy and was perfected in the narrative *Il*

Cortegiano (*The Courtier*) by Baldassare Castiglione. Published in Italian in 1528, the book was subsequently translated into English by Thomas Hoby and published in 1561 and 1588. It served to fix a standard of manners, not entirely new to England, in which courtesy was based on a beautiful purity of heart and was regarded as a manifestation of the highest good.

The perfect gentleman (or courtier) was a passionate friend, for "that high degree of friendship," Castiglione wrote, "ministereth unto us all the goodness contained in our life. . . . I would have our courtier, therefore, to find him out an especial and hearty friend, if it were possible. . . ." Antonio's friendship is combined with other noble characteristics, as we shall see, all of which add up to a portrait of Antonio as a perfect Renaissance gentleman.

Bassanio hesitates to divulge his plan. By way of introduction he tells Antonio how, when he was a boy, he often lost an arrow by carelessly shooting it without looking to see which way it went. When this happened, he sometimes managed to retrieve the arrow by firing another after it in the same direction, but this time keeping careful watch on its flight. In any case, if he did not find the first arrow, at least he did not lose the second. Turning to the matter at hand, he tells Antonio, "I owe you much, and like a willful youth / That which I owe is lost; but if you please / To shoot another arrow that self way / Which you did shoot the first, I do not doubt, / As I will watch the aim, or to find both / Or bring your latter hazard back again / And thankfully rest debtor for the first."

Antonio chides his friend for this elaborate preparation and tells Bassanio that there is nothing he would not do for him. Thus encouraged, Bassanio reverts to the subject of the lady, which is how their conversation started. He tells Antonio that "In Belmont is a lady richly left;/ And she is fair, and fairer than that word,/ Of wondrous virtues." This lady is Portia, whom Bassanio met some time ago in Belmont and from whose eyes he received "fair speechless messages" that she would not be averse to his suit. Like the Portia of Ancient Rome (daughter of Cato and wife of Brutus), she is an extraordinary woman. Suitors flock to her from all over the world, just as the mythological heroes sought the Golden Fleece. (In Greek mythology the Golden Fleece on the island of Colchis was a precious object for which many men went in quest. Jason finally obtained it after overcoming great danger.) Bassanio tells Antonio that he is sure that if he had the means to return to Belmont he, like Jason, would win the prize so many men seek.

Antonio immediately agrees to help his friend, but, with several ships at sea, he does not have the necessary cash on hand. He therefore asks Bassanio to find someone who will lend the money on the basis of Antonio's.

COMMENT: Antonio and Bassanio are alike in many ways. Both show the virtues and characteristics of the Renaissance gentleman who engages in perfect friendship. Antonio is apparently older than Bassanio since he has been able to lend his friend money in his youth, and he is certainly at this point a more melancholy soul than the gregarious and romantic Bassanio. Like the speaker in Shakespeare's famous sonnet series to a young friend, Antonio appears to idolize Bassanio and shows that he is capable of the extraordinarily devoted and selfless friendship of an older man. Bassanio, still in his prime, is interested in the lady of Belmont whom he describes as a perfect Renaissance lady.

The interests of the two friends are readily explained by the precepts of love described in Castiglione's Courtier. Neo-Platonic Christian philosophy of the Renaissance recognized three stages of love in man. The first and most youthful level was sensual love, a manifestation of youthful appetite, which if directed toward a virtuous lady informed the youth of the nature of love and prepared him for the second stage of devolopment. In the second stage, Reason prevailed and manifested itself in friendship and in the decline of youthful appetite. The third and final stage of love pertained to the Understanding and could only be found among angels in the world of the the spirit.

Bassanio is clearly at the first stage of development, and Antonio at the second. His interest in promoting Bassanio's suit with the lady of Belmont would be to direct his friend in the course by which perfect love eventually could be achieved.

In the course of their conversation, we learn about Portia for the first time in the play. The conversation works as a preparation for the following scene in which Portia appears personally. She is both fair and wondrously virtuous and is sought by suitors from all over the Mediterranean world. But first of all, she is a lady "richly left," an heiress of great wealth. Bassanio's interest in the lady's fortune has disturbed critics who are ill-informed about Renaissance social history. Bassanio is simply acting in accordance with the humanist code of behavior (of the sort drawn up by Castiglione in *The Courtier*), which exepected a person of a given rank, education, appearance, and sex to conduct himself in accordance with the rules drawn up for his class. Bassanio is the descendant of a noble Venetian family, and in his schooldays displayed that "certain Recklessness" or nonchalance about money which was the hallmark of gentle birth. Now that he has ended that stage of his youth, it is incumbent upon him to marry a lady appropriate to his class, to restore the fortune he has squandered, and to repay his old debts. It is to Bassanio's credit, therefore, and in accordance with "nature," that he take an interest in Portia's wealth and be concerned over his debt to Antonio.

SUMMARY. The first scene of the first act prepares us for what is to follow. We meet most of the main characters of the play and hear about one other, Portia. We learn the following important things:

1. Antonio is a rich merchant who has many ships embarked on trading ventures on the seas. He is marked at once as a melancholy man, a "humorous" type who is expected to follow a line of behavior already familiar to the Elizabethan audience. He is a reflective man, given to a few words, a devoted friend, an idealist, and one who cares little for the material things of this world. He is also quick to anger (as we shall soon learn) and staunch in his submissiveness to melancholy (and later, to misfortune).

2. Salarino and Salanio's speeches serve to explicate the character of Antonio and to establish the atmosphere of Venice as an opulant city, thriving on commerce.

3. The loquacious Gratiano shows a rather crude and ready wit. What he says appears to be nonsense, but is actually extremely informative satire of the types of mankind. He calls himself a fool and serves as contrast to the much wiser Antonio whom he warns against appearing as a pseudo-wise man.

4. Lorenzo says very little, suggesting that he is a worthy gentlemen. (Garrulous types are obviously comic characters.) He too is contrasted by Gratiano. We shall see more of him later.

5. Bassanio's character is established in connection with Antonio and Portia. He is the worthy object of Antonio's devotion in that, having squandered his fortune and fallen into debt, he is now ready to make amends for his earlier profligacy by forming an alliance with a lady of virtue and wealth through whom his own character and fortune will be improved.

6. The plot is put into motion in this scene. We learn that Bassanio wants to go to Belmont to woo the rich, beautiful, and virtuous Portia, and that Antonio agrees to borrow money to finance his trip to Belmont. The major action of the play will revolve around (1) Bassanio's wooing of Portia and (2) Antonio's borrowing money for his friend from a cruel usurer.

Act One, Scene Two

The scene is Belmont. Portia and her waiting woman, Nerissa, are talking. "By my troth, Nerissa, my little body is aweary of this great world," sighs Portia, but Nerissa, instead of commiserating with her mistress, declares that Portia's unhappiness can only be the result of an overabundance of good fortune. It is a fact, she says, that superfluity can be as oppressive as insufficiency: "they are as sick that surfeit with too much as they that starve with nothing." The ideal in all things is the mean between two extremes. Portia approves of these "Good sentences and well pronounced," but regrets that it is easier to give good advice than to follow it. I can easier teach twenty what were good to be done," she declares, "than to be one of the twenty to follow mine own teaching. The brain may devise laws for the blood, but a hot temper leaps o'er a cold decree."

The knowledge that one *ought* to be happy is never the same as actually *being* happy, which Portia says she is not. And the reason that she is not happy becomes clear when she adds that all this talk will not serve to choose her a husband. After all, she sighs, it is not up to her to choose a husband for herself. According to her father's instructions laid down just before he died, suitors for her hand must choose which of three caskets contains her picture. Portia finds it hard to bear that she is "curbed by the will of a dead father," that she may neither accept nor refuse any man on the basis of her own inclination, but Nerissa consoles her with the assurance that dying men often have good inspirations. She tells Portia that her father must have devised the lottery in such a way that only a man truly worthy of her would be able to choose correctly.

> **COMMENT:** Portia is the first lady among Shakespeare's great heroines, one of his "characters of intellect," as Mrs. Jameson called her in *Shakespeare Heroines* (1833). She is a woman of wit, imagination, intelligence, humor, resourcefulness, sensibility, and compassion, a perfect Renaissance lady. In her first scene, we learn that she is "aweary of this great world," which immediately associates her with Antonio, who is so sad that "it wearies me." (I.i). We may understand this weariness to mean that Portia is also a reflective person who values spiritual things above others. Unlike Antonio, however, the source of her disturbance lies in her recognition of her own powers of reasoning, which she feels enable her to choose her own husband, and her virtuous desire to remain obedient to her dead father's wish that her husband be selected by the means he has devised. She learns as the play progresses the wisdom of her father's commandment.
>
> Nerissa is a confidente-servant, a popular type in Renaissance literature. She is companion or lady-in-waiting to Portia and acts as a foil to the heroine of the play. She plays the realist to Portia's idealist, and is bright and witty in the same way but not to the same degree as her mistress. She plays an amusing part in advancing the comic theme of servants who imitate their masters.

Nerissa questions Portia about her feelings towards the numerous suitors who have already presented themselves in Belmont and, while she acknowledges that "it is a sin to be a mocker," Portia takes the opportunity to poke fun at them one by one. First there is the Neapolitan prince, who talks of nothing but his horse and of his own expertize in shoeing him. Portia gaily wonders if perhaps "my lady his mother played false with a smith." Next there is the County (Count) Palatine, whose particular characteristic is a perpetual frown. Since he never smiles now in his youth, Portia concludes that he will undoubtedly be "the weeping philosopher when he grows old." She declares she would rather be married to "a death's head with a bone in his mouth than to either of these."

The Neapolitan and the Palatine are Italian noblemen. The next four suitors are French, English, Scottish, and German. Of the Frenchman

Portia declares, I know God made him, and therefore let him pass for a man," but she thinks he has no character at all, for he changes mood and behavior from minute to minute. As for the Englishman, Portia cannot really judge, because he knows neither Latin, French, nor Italian (all of which, presumably, she does know), and she has only a smattering of English. Consequently, they cannot carry on any sort of conversation. His appearance, however, she finds decidely peculiar, for he looks as if he bought his coat in Italy, his breeches in France, his hat in Germany, and "his behavior everywhere." The Scottish lord is not worth much comment. Portia merely remarks mockingly that he seems to be generous, for when the Englishman gave him a box on the ear he swore he would pay him back. Finally, as for the German, Portia makes fun of his love of drink, but declares she dislikes him as much in the morning, when he is sober, as in the evening, when he is drunk."

COMMENT: It is interesting to note that this scene is in prose rather than in poetry. As a general rule, the characters involved in the main action of a Shakespearean play speak in blank verse (unrhymed iambic pentameter), while the characters of the comic subplot speak in prose. In all her other appearances in the play, Portia speaks in blank verse, but in this scene she engages in satire, drawing verbal caricatures of her suitors, although she knows "it is a sin to be a mocker." Thus, she speaks prose, the language deemed most suitable for satire and comedy, according to Renaissance practice.

Portia's suitors come from all over the world, for her fame has spread throughout Europe, and this gives Shakespeare a chance to poke fun at some national weakspots. Thus, the French suitor is flighty, the German is a drunkard, and the Scotsman is subject to the Englishman. As for the English lord, he is mocked for knowing no foreign languages and for his motley attire. These caricatures, incidentally, are microcosmic prose essays of the sort which were popularized by the "character-writers" early in the seventeenth century. Similar comic national types appeared with some frequency in the comic or antimasque sections of court masques produced during the reigns of King James and Charles.

When Portia has run through the list, Nerissa comforts her with the news that she need not fear marrying any of these gentlemen, who have all decided to return home rather than risk the condition imposed by her father's will on all her suitors. (This condition, we will later learn, is that before he may choose among the caskets, each suitor must swear that if he chooses wrongly he will never seek to marry another woman. Portia is delighted to hear this, and says. "There is not one among them but I dote on his very absence."

Nerissa asks if Portia remembers one man in particular, "a Venetian, a scholar, and a soldier," who came to visit during her father's lifetime. This man, declares the maid, seemed more deserving than any other of winning a fair lady. Portia does indeed remember him; his name is Bassanio, and he did seem worthy of all praise. At this moment a messenger enters with news that the current batch of suitors is departing and that the Prince of Morocco will arrive shortly as a new suitor. The lady of Belmont wishes she could feel as happy to see the new suitor arrive as she is glad to see the old ones leave.

COMMENT: Portia's criticism of her suitors is both witty and astute. She is too intelligent and well-educated to enjoy the company of humorless men or men with limited interests. Bassanio, on the other hand, is "a Venetian, a scholar, and a soldier." He is the perfect gentleman, in short, and as Nerissa tells us, he is worthy of a fair lady. This description of Bassanio is reminiscent of another admirable hero, which Shakespeare created some years later. Hamlet, the noble Prince of Denmark, had "the courtier's, soldier's, scholar's eye, tongue, sword." (III.i.159), we may recall. The tendency in Shakespeare to associate chains of words and ideas makes if fairly certain that Bassanio, like Hamlet later, was intended as the perfect gentleman.

As a scholar, Bassanio can be expected to use language with great wit, to pun and jest ironically with the best of them (Portia). As a soldier, of course, he has been brave and bold, skilled in the use of weapons, physically alert, admirable in every way in the eyes of the fair lady of the Renaissance ideal. Other courteous traits are implied in Nerissa's description of Bassanio. He will be a passionate friend, a humble suppliant, and a totally dedicated lover. He can be counted on to "hazard all" and choose the leaden casket.

SUMMARY. This scene is important for the following reasons:

1. We meet Portia, and begin to appreciate her fine qualities. She is not very happy in her present position, waiting for one of her numerous suitors to choose correctly among the caskets in order to marry her, but in the meantime she makes the best of her wit by satirizing her suitors.
2. Nerissa, Portia's maid, is also very clever, but her part is decidedly subordinate to that of the mistress. Nerissa's chief function in the drama is being the foil against which Portia's character, particularly her wit, is revealed.

3. In Portia's prose descriptions of her suitors, Shakespeare satirizes the outstanding national foibles of England, France, Germany, and Scotland.

4. We learn that Portia remembers Bassanio very well and with very fond memories. Nerissa agrees with her that he is the kind of man whose suit would be acceptable.

5. The Prince of Morocco is on his way to try his luck. We will see in the next act how well he fares.

Act One, Scene Three

The scene is back in Venice. Bassanio has found Shylock, a Jewish moneylender, and is seeking to borrow three thousand ducats for three months, for which Antonio will be bound. As Bassanio tells him the sum of money required and the length of time. Shylock repeats the words in a noncommittal fashion: "Three thousand ducats, well . . . For three months, well . . . Antonio shall become bound, well." Pressed for a decision by Bassanio, who is becoming impatient, the moneylender finally says, "Antonio is a good man." Bassanio, evidently thinking that Shylock uses the word "good" in its moral sense, asks indignantly if he has heard anything to the contrary about his friend, but Shylock assures him that by "good" he simply meant that Antonio has good credit. However, continues Shylock, Antonio is not a very safe risk, since his fortune is bound up in commercial ventures at sea, which is not entirely safe, for "ships are but boards, sailors but men; there be land rats and water rats, water thieves and land thieves–I mean pirates" (pun on pie rats). On the whole, however, Shylock decides that Antonio is sufficient, but he insists on speaking to the merchant himself.

COMMENT: Shylock is one of the most fascinating and one of the most controversial characters in Shakespeare. Critics at one extreme have argued that Shakespeare intended Shylock as the stereotype of the infidel Jews, and a complete villain. Critics at the other extreme contend that Shylock is a tragic figure, more sinned against than sinning. In this scene we are introduced to him for the first time, and we must watch carefully what he says and how he says it in order to decide what sort of person he really is.

Perhaps, the first thing we notice about Shylock is that he was probably costumed like the conventional comic Jew is earlier morality plays, in which Judas Iscariot, the betrayer of Christ and the most debased of villains, appeared in a red beard, red wig, long nose, and "gaberdine," and was immediately identified by his stereotyped attire. Shylock considers Bassanio's request with slow deliberation, repeating everything that Bassanio says as if stalling for time to weigh the pros and cons within himself. Shylock evidently keeps abreast of the business affairs of the principal merchants of Venice, for he already knows how many ships Antonio has at sea and what their destinations are. He is wary and pragmatic. Thus, when he uses the word "good," his meaning is entirely financial, whereas for Bassanio, whose orientation is neo-Platonic and Christian, the word "good" is primarily a moral category. Another important difference between these two men is their manner of speech. Shylocks' repetition of certain words and phrases is partly comic and partly ominous, as is his warning about land rats and water rats. In the light of future developments regarding Antonio's ships, his forebodings are particularly significant. On the whole, in this opening discussion, Shylock appears as a highly cautious and suspicious individual, which the Elizabethan imagined a Jew to be.

Bassanio invites Shylock to meet Antonio at dinner, a suggestion that Shylock takes very badly. "Yes," he says sarcastically, "to smell pork, to eat of the habitation which your prophet the Nazarite conjured the devil into." He declares that he will do business with Christians, walk with them, talk with them, but he refuses to eat with them, drink with them, or pray with them.

> **COMMENT:** The Elizabethan audience had already identified Shylock as the comic Jew of the play by the costume he wore. It was prepared to enjoy jokes at the expense of this character, who, as in Marlowe's well-known *The Jew of Malta,* was a moneylender or usurer, an occupation held only by Jews. It was amusing to Shakespeare's audiences that Shylock only thinks of "goodness" in terms of worldly goods; it was part of the Christian stereotype of the Jew to see him this way. The stereotype is continued in a jest on Jewish dietary law forbidding the consumption of "unclean" meat, which was the subject of vulgar amusement in Christian art and legend throughout the Middle Ages and Renaissance. Shylock displays the scorn of Christian doctrine attributed to the Jews by sarcastically referring to "your prophet the Nazarite" (Matthew 2:23) and to Jesus' exorcism of the devils, which possessed the two demoniacs, by transferring them to a herd of swine, which he then drove into the sea (Matthew 8:28-33). That Shylock refers to Christ by one of his *New Testament* sobriquets is a sign of the Jew's refusal to acknowledge Jesus as the Christ (Messiah, the Lord's anointed). His rejection of Basanio's dinner invitation is couched in terms of the anti-Christ.
>
> Bassanio's invitation is meant as a friendly gesture, and Shylock's reply (if heard by Bassanio) is hostile and discourteous. One editor of the play suggests that Shylock's remarks about pork and his reference to "your prophet" were probably spoken in an aside (a speech which is intended only for the audience's hearing). In any case, the speech reveals Shylock's hostility toward the Christian world, for he assumes that Bassanio intends to flout his religious traditions.

Just at this moment along comes Antonio himself, and Shylock, noticing him out of the corner of his eye, expresses in an aside (that merchant looks like a "fawning publican." "I hate him for he is a Christian; / But more, for that in low simplicity/ He lends out money gratis and brings down/ The rate of usance here with us in Venice. / If I can catch him once upon the hip,/ I will feed fat the ancient grudge I bear him." Shylock goes on to say that Antonio "hates our sacred nation," and concludes, "Cursed be my tribe/ If I forgive him."

> **COMMENT:** Shylock's aside continues the unflattering portrait of the Jewish usurer as a greedy, rapacious, revengeful, and proud man. Antonio's humility, his resemblance to a "fawning publican" (Luke 18:10-14), enrages Shylock. In fact, he hates Antonio because

he practices Christian generosity and humanity, lends money without interest (see Matthew 5:42), and competes with the professional usurers of Venice. The themes of pride vs. humility, hate vs. love, thrift vs. usury, are introduced at this point.

Other recurrent themes suggested in this speech by Shylock are mercy, revenge, and cannibalism. Shylock plans to take revenge against Antonio if he can "catch him one upon the hip," that is, if he can get him at his mercy, and he swears by his tribe that he will not forgive Antonio for denouncing him to the merchants of Venice. Shylock also promises to "feed fat the ancient grudge," suggesting for the first of many times in this play, the disgusting connotation of cannibalism. (Charges that Jews practiced ritual murder and drank the blood of Christians during their religious ceremonies and that they desecrated the wafer—the body of Chirst—for the same purpose, were regularly made during the Middle Ages.)

The hatred and desire for revenge which Shylock reveals, and the humility and Christian idealism which Shylock correctly attributes to Antonio, have their counterparts in medieval and Renaissance Christian doctrine. Pauline Christianity, which formed the basis of this doctrine, ignored the evolution of Hellenist-Judaism from hide-bound literalism to the more spiritual form of worship which anticipated Jesus' teachings and formed the basis of Jesus' precepts. Thus, the God of the *Old Testament* was commonly viewed as a vengeful God who had demanded "eye for eye, tooth for tooth, hand for hand, foot for foot" (Exodus 21:24), while the God of the *New Testament* was seen as a merciful one: "Ye have heard that it hath been said, An eye for an eye, and a tooth for a tooth: But I say unto you, That ye resist not evil: but whosoever shall smite thee on they right cheek, turn to him the other also" (Matthew 5:38-9). Shylock here represents the spirit of the *Old Testament*, while Antonio represents the spirit of the New; they symbolize the doctrines of hate vs. love, revenge vs. forgiveness, usury vs. charity.

While speaking to the audience in an aside, Shylock pretends that he has not seen Antonio but has been thinking about how he can raise the necessary sum of money. He looks up from his revery and says that, although he does not have the ready cash, his friend Tubal can supply the rest, so there will be no problem. Suddenly he notices Antonio (who has been standing there for several minutes) and greets him in sycophantic terms, addressing him as "Your worship," and saying, "Rest you fair, good signoir./ Your worship was the last man in our mouths."

COMMENT: Shylock's last line continues the idea of cannibalism, which had begun in his aside and which suggests that his thoughts are inhuman and evil. Shylock's ability to dissemble his feelings is amply demonstrated in his gracious reception of Antonio, whom he has just been vilifying. We must keep in mind this hypocrisy when we hear Shylock tell Antonio and Bassanio later in this scene that he wants to be friends with them. Shylock's hyprocrisy carries on the theme of anti-Judaism (see Matthew 23:28) and is related to the theme of deceptive appearances, which forms the crux of the romantic plot, the choosing of the caskets.

Antonio does not beat around the bush with Shylock but goes directly to the point. Although as a rule he neither lends nor borrows money at interest, he is ready to break his custom in this case in order to help a friend. Shylock justifies his financial practices by citing the story from the Book of Genesis (30:31-43) in the Bible of how Jacob dealt with his uncle Laban. It was agreed between the two men that when Laban's flocks gave birth, Jacob would take as his wages all the multicolored lambs, leaving the solid colored lambs for Laban. While the rams and ewes were mating, however, Jacob used a special magic device to make sure that all the lambs would be spotted and speckled, and in this way he got the best of the bargain. Shylock approves of Jacob's apparent cunning, and declares, "This was a way to thrive, and he was blest;/ And thrift is blessing if men steal it not." Antonio declares that it was beyond Jacob's power to determine the color of lambs before conception, and that their complexion was the work of God, not man. He does not see that this story will justify the practice of usury, and Shylock answers simply that he can make money breed as fast as rams and ewes (which is comic). Antonio remarks to Bassanio apropos of this discussion that "The devil can cite Scripture for his purpose," for Shylock hides his villainous deeds behind the holy words of the Bible, whose meaning he distorts. "O, what a goodly outside falsehood hath!" Antonio observes.

COMMENT: What Shakespeare fails to include in Shylock's story of Jacob and Laban is that Laban deceived and cheated Jacob first by removing all the speckled kine from the flock before Jacob could collect them. The Jewish meaning of this analogy between Laban, Jacob and the usurer is that Christians, like Laban, restricted Jews from ordinary means of earning a living (relegating many of them to the business of usury and despising them for conducting this business on a profitable basis), but the usurer, like Jacob, has foiled his Christian deceivers. Antonio points out that Jacob's profits were achieved by the means of God's intervention and were blessed rewards for years of honest labor as Laban's shepherd. He feels that Shylock, by putting his money to work for him and by charging interest for loans, profits from another man's need, not from his own labor. Jewish and Christian interpretations of the Scriptures differed then, as now, and Antonio's comment about the devil citing Scripture expresses the Christian view of Jewish biblical interpreters. the theme of deceptive appearances in Antonio's last remark applies to Shylock's alleged misuse of the Bible.

Shakespeare also engages in a play on word "kind," using it with different meanings during this scene. The word-play is calculated to associate Shylock with carnality, and Antonio and Bassanio with generosity.

Shylock describes ewes and rams (creatures Shakespeare usually associated with lust) as "doing the deed of kind" ("deed of nature," that is, "breeding"), and he thinks of money as a thing capable of breeding or multiplying. Later in the scene, Shylock will offer "kind" (apparently "generosity," but with lustful connotations), and Bassanio will be suspicious of Shylock's offer.

Returning to the matter at hand, Antonio asks Shylock, who has been computing the rate of interest, whether or not he will supply the money. For answer Shylock complains in a long and bitter speech about the hostile and contemptuous way that Antonio has long treated him in public. "In the Rialto you have rated me . . . you call me misbeliever, cutthroat dog, /And spit upon my Jewish gaberdine, / And all for use of that which is mine own." After such words and such treatment, says Shylock, is there any reason why he should be courteous and obliging? "Hath a dog money?" Shylock asks. Is it not too ironical for him to whisper humbly, "Fair sir, you spit on me on Wednesday last, / You spurned me such a day, another time / You called me dog; and for these courtesies / I'll lend you thus much moneys?"

Antonio replies that he is just as likely to call Shylock dog again and to spurn him again. He tells the moneylender that although he holds Antonio as an enemy, Shylock may still lend him money for his own profit. Friends do not charge interest (which Antonio calls "a breed for barren metal"). It is better to lend money at interest to an enemy, in any case, for then one may exact the penalty later with "better face."

COMMENT: In computing his interest "rate," Shylock is reminded of how Antonio "rated" (berated) him in the marketplace. Shakespeare once again shows (see Salarino's speech in I.i) how any word or idea may serve as a reminder of an emotional or mental preoccupation which has been momentarily forgotten.

Shylock is obsessed by Antonio's vilifications, which, ironically, he calls "courtesies." Four times in a single speech, he repeats Antonio's dog-epithet. Dog was a common Christian metaphor for Jew, and Antonio's abuse is not an unusual one in his world. Shylock's explanation of his hatred, however, is a unique expression; the Jew in earlier literature was never given such an opportunity to state his grievances. In view of Antonio's abuses, it is small wonder that Romantic and subjective critics decide that Shylock was more sinned against than sinning, and it is no surprise that Shakespeare idolaters refuse to believe the great Bard could have approved of Antonio's cruelty to the moneylender.

Antonio's character has been called into question by Shylock's description of his abuses. Antonio admits that he has humiliated the Jew and that he will do it again. But this is not inconsistent with his character as a perfect Renaissance gentleman, which included, among other virtues, devotion to the Christian faith and scorn for "misbelievers." In addition, Antonio is a melancholy man, and it should not be forgotten that his nature had an irascible side too.

The play on "kind" and 'breed" is continued in Antonio's metaphor for "interest," the unnatural profit extracted from "barren metal," which by nature is incapable of breeding. Antonio's argument that money lent to an enemy may be exacted with "better face" is another statement of the theme of hypocricy or deceptive appearancs. To Antonio, it is hypocrisy to charge interest and still claim friendship.

After Antonio's outburst Shylock suddenly changes his tone, and declares that he wants to be friends with Antonio, to forget the past, and to supply the three thousand ducats at no interest. "This is kind I offer." Bassanio, suspicious, exclaims "This were kindness," and Shylock goes on to explain that all they need to do is accompany him to a notary to sign a bond "in merry sport" that if Antonio does not repay three thousand ducats in three months he will forfeit a pound of flesh, to be cut off and taken from what part of his body pleases Shylock. Antonio agrees to sign such a bond, "And say there is much kindness in the Jew," but Bassanio is appalled at the proposed condition. Antonio reassures him that the bond will not be forfeited, since his ships will certainly return well before three months with three times the value of the bond. Shylock declares that the bond is just a kind of joke, since he could make no profit from a pound of human flesh, as he would from a pound of mutton or beef or goat flesh. These Christians, he says, suspect the intentions of others because of their own hard hearts. He insists that he is doing this as a favor and in friendship, and says, "for my love I pray you wrong me not." These words settle the matter for Antonio. They agree to meet at the notary's, where Antonio will give instruction for the bond to be drawn up. Shylock returns home to get the money and to check up on his household left in the care of his servant, "an unthrifty knave." When the Jew has left, Antonio cheerfully tells Bassanio, "The Hebrew will turn Christian; he grows kind," but Bassanio, who distrusts Shylock, answers, "I like not fair terms and a villain's mind." Antonio, however, certain that his ships will come home a month before the bond is due, refuses to be dismayed.

COMMENT: The theme of deceptive appearances is augmented by dramatic ambiguity of these last speeches created by Shakespeare's skillfully ironic use of words with double meanings. There is very little doubt, however, about Shakespeare's intentions. Exigencies of the plot and theme, combined with Renaissance Christian values, point to a single plausible interpretation of this section of the scene.

Shylock offers "kind," a word which suggests "generosity and friendship," but which also suggests "engendering in nature." The sort of engendering the Jew is supposed to believe in, however, is the unnatural breeding of gold and silver. By association of ideas, Shylock is an unnatural man (one who interpreted Scriptures with the devil's tongue and one who has already been linked with carnality). Bassanio is suspicious of Shylock's offer of "kind" and rephrases the offer by substituting the conditional verb "were" for Shylock's "is" and a less ambiguous form of the word "kind," that is, "kindness." Bassanio means, in effect: Yes, Shylock, your offer would be a kindness if the "kind" you speak of were Christian "kindness." I fear, however, that you are using the word in its carnal sense, for Jews are a fleshly race and have no idea of the spirit of the word which means "generosity." Shylock confirms Bassanio's suspicion when he demonstrates the "kindness" he has in mind; it is the offer of the flesh-bond. Shylock's next speech is full of fleshly imagery: "man's flesh," "flesh of muttons, beef, or goats." The theme of cannibalism or carnality is repeated over and over again, even as Shylock chastises Christians (not just Bassanio for their suspicious natures.

Antonio is surprised to find "kindness" (generosity and, perhaps, nature) in a Jew, but he is willing to accept it as possible, partly because he is extremely anxious to help his friend Bassanio and partly because, like other Christians of his age, he is still hopeful that "the Hebrew will turn Christian." It is clear the Shylock uses the words "kind" and "kindness" ironically, that he expects the Christians to believe he means "generosity" when he actually has in mind a carnal and cannibalistic transaction involving the flesh-bond.

Bassanio has picked up Shylock's reference to his servant as an "unthrifty knave." We shall see shortly that Bassanio interprets Shylock's "unthrifty" as "Christian generosity" and regards Shylock's ill favor as a good recommendation for Launcelot.

The theme of deceptive appearances is once more asserted in Bassanio's interpretation of Shylock and his offer as "fair terms and a villain's mind," and this may be taken as an instance of dramatic foreshadowing, a device frequently found in Shakespeare, by which subsequent events of the plot are anticipated.

SUMMARY. This scene is extremely important for the following reasons:

1. The plot is advanced when we meet Shylock, the Jewish usurer from whom Bassanio borrows three thousands ducats with a pound of Antonio's flesh as security.

2. The *Old* and *New Testament*, Jewish vs. Christian dispute, which underscores both plots in the play, is introduced in the debate between Shylock and Antonio over the interpretation of Jacob's wand.

3. The characterization of Shylock is presented along the lines of the Renaissance stereotype of the Jew as a "dog," a usurer, an anti-Christ, and a revengeful, hateful, hypocritical, carnal, and cannibalistic "devil."

4. The friendship theme is advanced in the generous behavior of Antonio and Bassanio to each other.

Act Two, Scene One

Back in Belmont, the Prince of Morocco (described in the stage directions as a "tawny Moor all in white") is pressing his suit to Portia. He explains that his skin is dark because of the climate of his country and hopes that she will not object to him on that account. The blood that runs in his veins, he assures her, is redder than that of "the fairest creatures northward born," and the most beautiful ladies of Morocco are in love with him. Therefore, he would not change the color of his skin except in order to win Portia's favor.

Portia, for her part, declares that she is bound to abide by her father's order regarding the caskets irrespective of her inclinations. However, she tells him that if the choice were hers to make she would not be led by superficial matters of appearance, and that he would be as likely a choice as any suitor who has yet come to Belmont.

COMMENT: The aspect of the tawny Moor in his flowing white robes appealed to the Elizabethans' interest in exotic places and manners, but it also appealed to their sense of humor. Elizabethans did not distinguish between Negroes and Moors; both were regarded as members of strange barbaric races not far removed from savagery, cannabilism, and carnality, which the red blood symbolizes. Their complexion was both feared and abhorred, and marriage between a Moor and a Christian lady was regarded as unnatural and impossible. If he chooses correctly, however, Portia will marry the Moor in spite of his appearance, for his correct choice would prove his inner worth. But that this Moor should sue for Portia's hand is a completely ridiculous notion and is characteristic of his shallow, presumptuous, and boastful disposition. The Moor lacks the humility and spiritual sensibilty to choose wisely.

Portia finds the Prince extremely distasteful, although she seems to treat him with courtesy, for her discourteous retort is covered by a witty irony, which the thick-headed Moor is unable to comprehend. Elizabethans shared Portia's distaste for Moors and applauded her ironically witty assurance to Morocco that she likes him as well as her previous suitors, which means not at all.

The theme of deceptive appearances runs through the scene and is expressed, for example, in Portia's assurance to the Moor that she is not led solely by "nice direction of a maiden's eyes."

The Prince thanks her for these words and says he is ready to be led to the caskets to make his choice. He only wishes that his fortune depended on his courage rather than on mere luck (it depends on neither), for he swears that in order to win Portia he would stare down the sternest eyes, outbrave the most daring heart, steal cubs from a she-bear, or mock an angry lion (yet he refuses to hazard the leaden box). He brags about having slain the Shah of Persia as well as a Persian prince and about having won three victories over the Sultan Solyman. However, the fact remains that he must take his chance with the caskets, and before doing so, he must go to the temple to swear that if he chooses wrongly, he will never again ask a lady to marry him. The Prince, Portia, and the others go off to the temple.

> **COMMENT:** Oaths in the temple were expressly forbidden in Christian doctrine (Matthew 5:33-37), and Shylock's oath "by our holy Sabbath" is treated as a religious mockery. Yet Portia is party to Morocco's swearing.

SUMMARY. This brief scene is interesting and important for the following reasons:

1. The romantic plot of the caskets is advanced, and an interlude of high-comedy is provided as a gentle contrast to the iniquitous flesh-bond scene.

2. We are amused by the subtle and witty caricature of the Prince of Morocco which acts as a contrast to the grotesquely satirical portrait of Shylock the Jew.

3. We are given further evidence of Portia's wit, courtesy, and filial obedience as she equivocates with the Moor, obscures her distaste for him, yet admits she will marry him if he chooses the correct casket.

Act Two, Scene Two

The scene is Venice once again. Launcelot Gobbo (the servant whom Shylock, in Act One, Scene Three, called an "unthrifty knave"), enters alone. He is debating with himself whether or not to run away from his master, whom he cannot abide. On the one hand the devil tempts him to leave Shylock, and on the other hand his conscience bids him remain. "Well, my conscience says, 'Launcelot, budge not.' 'Budge,' says the fiend. 'Budge not,' says my conscience." The irony of the situation, says Launcelot, is that conscience counsels him to remain with the Jew, who is a kind of devil, whereas the devil himself bids him run from the Jew. After thinking it over, he decides that "The fiend gives the more friendly counsel. I will run, fiend; my heels are at your commandent; I will run."

> **COMMENT:** Launcelot Gobbo is the low-comedy clown in this scene, a type well-known in Italian *commedia,* where he was probably played as a hunchback or dwarf. (The name Gobbo is Italian for "crook't-backed," according to John Florio's Italian-English vocabulary of 1598). Renaissance audience found unnatural and misshapen creatures amusing in themselves, but the humor of physical appearance was only one of the kinds found in low-burlesque. Parody was another. Launcelot's opening speech is a mock debate of the kind frequently found in old morality plays in which

a misguided Christian, through examination of his conscience, finds his way back to the straight and narrow path.

Launcelot's reasoning is confused and digressive, but it ultimately brings him to the realization that since the Jew is "a kind of devil" (the word "kind again, meaning "sort" and by nature"), he should not serve him, although conscience ordinarily requires a man to give loyal service to his master. Instead, he will give in to the fiend (who counsels servants to be disloyal to their masters) and leave the Jew's service. Launcelot thinks he is serving the fiend by leaving the "devil," a thought which confuses him and amuses us.

Among his digressions is the first of Launcelot's allusions to illegitimacy; he calls himself "an honest man's son," then ludicrously qualifies his remmark; he is not so sure. Another source of humor in Launcelot's character is his tendency to mispronounce and misuse words. He speaks of Shylock as the devil's "incarnation," meaning "incarnate," for example. He is also the simple-minded victim of superstition and is terrified of demons, for a camparison of which, see Marlowe's scene between the clown and Wagner in *Doctor Faustus*.

At this moment of resolution, Old Gobbo, Launcelot's father, enters, coming from far away to see his son after a long time. Because he is almost totally blind, Gobbo does not recognize his son, and asks him for directions to Shylock's house. The playful Launcelot decides to have some fun with the old man for a while and gives him confusing direction which will cause him to turn and turn and turn. When the old man asks if Launcelot lives there, his son asks if he means "Master Launcelot," but Gobbo says Launcelot is "No master, sir, but a poor man's son." The clown insists they are talking of "Master Launcelot," and the old man maintains it is plain and simple Launcelot. Finally his son says that Master Launcelot is dead. Gobbo is stunned by this piece of news; he says that the boy was the prop and staff of his old age, which causes Launcelot to query the audience, "Do I look like a cudgel?"

COMMENT: In this highly comic exchange between father and son, several kinds of humor are employed. The dialogue as a whole is a parody of the classical recognition scene, in which long lost relatives were reunited in the most improbable ways. Lancelot, who has already demonstrated reasoning prowess of a fool, decides to try "confusion," using a malapropism for "conclusions" (an exercise in logic), with his father, and repeatedly abuses the word "ergo" (Latin for "therefore"). Jokes about pedantry in logic were common stock in Renaissance comedy. Launcelot's confusing directions to his father include instructions to "turn" ("take the devious route to evil" especially, "to comit adultery") (I.iii.79-80;III.iv,78-80) again and again, suggesting for the second time his father's promiscuous habits. The quibble over whether or not to call Launcelot "Master" is intended to expose the pig-headed literalness and pedantry of the simple old man, a country rustic (usually identified by a broad hat, cloak, and basket), and is a comic digression from Launcelot's jest, to make the old man cry, to "raise the waters" (with a probable pun on "urine").

At this point Lancelot decides to reveal his true identity. For a while he has a hard time convincing Gobbo, who cannot believe that this young man is really his son. However, Launcelot insists, "I am Launcelot—your boy that was, your son that is, and your child that shall be," and when he wins his point, for old Gobbo acknowledges him as his much-changed son with "what a beard thou got." He tells Launcelot that he has brought a present for Shylock, but the clown objects. "Give him a present?" he asks indignantly. Better "Give him a halter! I am famished in his service." Launcelot tells his father that he is determined to leave Shylock's service and to seek employment with Bassanio, who gives wonderful new liveries to his servants. He asks his father to give the present to Bassanio, whose service he wants to enter (for he is anxious to leave the Jew before he becomes one himself). Just at this moment, as luck would have it, along comes Bassanio in person.

COMMENT: After several further jests on the theme of illegitimacy Launcelot succeeds in convincing old Gobbo that he is his son. The old man fondles the youth's beard, remarking how greatly he has matured. Traditionally, the lines are accompanied by a farcial twist. Old Gobbo is made to stroke Launcelot's head as the youth kneels for his blessing.

Launcelot's description of his treatment by Shylock continues the sterotype of the Jew as an ungenerous and greedy miser who starves his servants. Launcelot's desire to leave Shylock before he becomes a Jew himself means that, as servants always imitate the manners of their masters, Launcelot will soon adopt the thrifty, ungenerous manners of the Jew. Servants' imitations of their masters were a popular comic theme in Shakespeare's plays (see Shallow and Davy in 2 *Henry IV*) and are echoed in the behavior of Gratiano and Nerissa.

Bassanio enters, accompanied by servants. He asks one of them to make sure that supper will be ready by five o'clock, to do some other errands, and to fetch Gratiano, for Bassanio is preparing to sail for Belmont shortly. Launcelot urges his father to go up to Basanio to request a position for his son. They approach Bassanio, but every time that old Gobbo starts to speak his son interrupts him to explain the situation in his own way. In this fashion and using a number of malapropisms, the two men talk and talk, but Bassanio can make nothing of their meaning. Old Gobbo gives him the present originally intended for Shylock (a dish of doves), and when Bassanio finally understands the nature of the request, he readily agrees to take Launcelot into his service, for Shylock (who had called Launcelot an "unthrifty knave") had unwittingly recommended his servant. Launcelot, for his part, states his preference for working with a Christian who had "the grace of God," rather than the Jew who simply has "enough" (in terms of worldly goods). Bassanio tells the clown to bid his old master farewell and orders that he be given a suit of livery more highly decorated than those of the other servants.

Launcelot is greatly pleased with his success. Looking at the palm of his hand, he pretends to read there a very satisfactory future for himself. "Here's a small trifle of wives! Alas, fifteen wives is nothing; a 'leven widows and nine maids is a small coming-in for one man. And then to scape drowning thrice." In great glee he goes off with his father to take leave of Shylock.

> **COMMENT:** The comedy again consists of the ridiculous mistakes in language and logic which Launcelot and his father make, and in the continued ridicule of Shylock as the stereotyped miserly Jew. Launcelot's complaints against his master prepare us for the dramatic presentation of the unbearable life led in the household of the close-fisted and puritanical usurer.
>
> Bassanio's willingness to hire Launcelot on the basis of Shylock's displeasure with his servant is a key to Bassanio's attitude toward Jews. He does not believe anything Shylock says and considers it a mark of virtue for Launcelot to be in Shylock's disfavor.
>
> After entering Bassanio's service, Launcelot, the rustic clown who misuses words, becomes a coarse duplication of his gentle and witty masters; he is then called a "wit-snapper," a sophisticated fool with "an army of good words" (III.v).

Bassanio gives some final orders to a servant named Leonardo concerning a feast that he will give tonight for his best friends. As Leonardo goes off, Gratiano appears and announces that he has a request. Without the least hesitation and without knowing what the request may be, Bassanio immediately replies, "You have obtained it." Gratiano then explains that he wants to go along to Belmont. Bassanio agrees, but asks his friend to moderate "with some cold drops of modesty" his "skipping spirit," lest his wild behavior give the wrong impression in Belmont of Bassanio's character. Gratiano readily agrees to put on a sober and pious expression and to act with utmost decorum. For this night, however, it is agreed that he will put on his "boldest suit of mirth," for there will be great merriment among the friends who will visit Bassanio at suppertime.

> **COMMENT:** Although it is unstated, Gratiano would like to travel with Bassanio because he cannot bear to be parted from his esteemed friend, whose every move he wishes to imiate. Gratiano is a kind of gentleman fool, who parallels the servant-fool Launcelot in seeking Bassanio's company. When Bassanio marries Portia, Gratiano marries her maid, and when Bassanio gives his ring to the disguised judge, Gratiano gives his to the judge's clerk. Humor is provided

by the imitative nature of fools and servants, and the Christian moral implicit in this comic theme is: a gentle master makes a gentle servant and an evil master makes devils of his followers. Gratiano, through Bassanio's gentle influence, curbs his loud ways to some extent. It is significant, however, that Gratiano can only emulate the surface of Bassanio's character; he cannot acquire its inner spirit (see Act IV).

As an ideal gentleman, Bassiano is unstintingly generous and obliging to his friends, and just as Antonio had granted his request for a loan, even before he had stated the nature of his request, so Bassanio grants Gratiano's suit without knowing what it is. This openhanded generosity and complete devotion to the ideal of friendship are designed as a sharp contrast to Shylock's mean spirit.

Gratiano's promised show of sobriety is really also an amusing caricature of the religous hyprocrite or puritan and implies that too many people—even those in Belmont—may judge a man by the appearance of his friend. In fact, Nerissa does just this later in the play, while the high-minded Portia wisely waits to see Gratiano's lord.

SUMMARY. This comic scene is amusing in itself, it also helps to move the plot along, and advances the themes of friendship and deceptive appearances.

1. Launcelot and Old Gobbo are introduced in this scene. The former will appear several times again.

2. Bassanio's suspicions about Shylock's generosity are confirmed by his hiring of Launcelot and his willingness to take Gratiano to Belmont.

3. The stereotype of Shylock as a miserly Jew is continued by Launcelot, and a caricature of a hypocritical or puritanical type is rendered by Gratiano.

4. The comic theme of servants who imitate their masters is introduced by Launcelot's defection to Bassanio and Gratiano's request to join Bassanio on his trip. It is underscored by the moral implication that servants and friends who are morally weak benefit from the guidance of noble Christian masters and friends.

Act Two, Scene Three

Launcelot has come to Shylock's house to say goodby to his former master. Jessica, the Jew's daughter, is there alone. She is very sorry that he is leaving. "Our house is hell," she declares, "and thou a merry devil / Didst rob it of some taste of tediousness." In parting she gives him a ducat and asks him to deliver a letter secretly to Lorenzo, who will be at Bassanio's house. Launcelot tearfully parts with her, calling her "most beautiful pagan, most sweet Jew!" He already suspects that a Christian (Lorenzo) has won her heart.

Launcelot leaves and Jessica, left alone, wonders what "heinous sin" it is that she is ashamed to be her father's child. Although she is his daughter by blood, she is completely alien to his way. She is secretly engaged to Lorenzo and, thinking of him, she swears aloud, "if thou keep promise, I shall end this strife, Become a Christian and thy loving wife!"

COMMENT AND SUMMARY. This brief scene introduces the beautiful and wistful Jessica. Her perfect spirit is displayed in her ability to recognize the "hell" of her Jewish household, to enjoy the jesting of Launcelot, whom she calls a "merry devil," and to love Lorenzo, a Christian.

She shares Launcelot's desire for mirth, but more than that, she shares his conflicting loyalties between conscience and the fiend. She is apparently torn by the desire to leave her father's house and go with Lorenzo and the desire to follow her conscience, which tells her that filial disloyalty is a "heinous sin." The same moral confiict which received comic treatment in Launcelot's opening scene is given pathos here when uttered by the disaffected "pagan" Jessica.

Filial loyalty, another moral theme in the play, has already been introduced by Portia, who has been made melancholy by her obligation to obey her father's will. The theme receives further examination in the plight of Jessica. The reasoning may seem obscure to the modern mind, but in Shakespeare's thought it was conceivable that Jessica could betray her Jewish father and still remain a pillar of virtue, while the Christian Portia, as a sign of her virtue, must remain firm in the performance of a daughter's duty. Symbolically, Jessica seeks release from the damnation of the Jews and looks for salvation in Christianity. From this theological point of view, Jessica's "betrayal" of Shylock is really an act of Christian virtue and faith; her obedience to a heavenly Father supercedes the necessity to obey her father in the flesh.

Act Two, Scene Four

Lorenzo, Gratiano, Salarino, and Salanio are making plans for the evening's masque. Gratiano complains that they have not made good preparation, and Salanio declares that it is better not to have any masque at all unless it is "Quaintly ordered." Lorenzo assures his friends that two hours are sufficient time for them to find torchbearers.

Launcelot arrives with Jessica's letter for Lorenzo, who immediately recognizes the fair handwriting. The clown is on his way to "bid my old master the Jew to sup to-night with my new master the Christian." (We already know that Bassanio plans to feast all his best acquaintance this evening.) Lorenzo gives Launcelot some money and asks him to assure Jessica that he will come by on time, for she is to be his torchbearer in disguise this evening.

Salarino and Salanio exit with Launcelot. Lorenzo, left alone with Gratiano, reveals the plan for his elopement with Jessica that night. Jessica has a page's suit in which she will dress up, and she will take with her gold and jewels from her father's house when she leaves. "If e'er the Jew her father come to heaven, / It will be for his gentle daughter's sake."

COMMENT AND SUMMARY. This brief scene moves the action of the play along and engages an interest in the subplot, which concerns Jessica's elopement with Lorenzo.

The masque planned for the evening's entertainment was a semi-dramatic spectacle of ancient origin in which music was a major element. The participants donned disguises and rode or marched in procession to their destination and there performed dances, songs, or pantomines, usually of an allegorical nature. Masques "after the manner of Italy" became especially popular in the court of Henry VIII and remained in vogue until Milton's time. Beside suggesting the contemporary manners of Italy, the masque planned in *The Merchant* (but never carried out) has a special value for the subplot in that Jessica can conveniently disguise as a page in order to elope with Lorenzo.

A number of loose ends in *The Merchant* suggest that it was a revision of an earlier play. The masque incident may have appeared in an early version, and we may imagine the comic interlude that might have been developed with Jessica carrying a torch at the dinner that her father Shylock attended.

Lorenzo's character is expanded in this brief scene. Already presented as a quiet man, he is seen here as a devoted and courtly lover, who can turn a figure in praise of his lady in the conventional and accepted phrases of Renaissance romance poetry. Jessica's hand is whiter than the paper on which her note is written, and she is the "gentle" (with a pun on "gentile) daughter of the Jew, who may yet win a place for her father in heaven (from which all Jews are banned).

Act Two, Scene Five

Launcelot has found Shylock just about to enter his house. The Jew warns his former servant that in Bassanio's service "Thou shalt not gormandize / As thou hast done with me," nor sleep and snore all day long. While saying this he has been calling his daughter, but when Launcelot comically echoes Shylock's call for Jessica, Shylock reproves him. "Who bids thee call? I do not bid thee call." And Launcelot remembers that Shylock always told him not to do anything without bidding.

Jessica enters and Shylock gives her his keys, saying that he is going out for supper. He broods about going. "I am not bid for love—they flatter me—/ And yet I'll go in hate to feed upon / The prodigal Christian." He is vaguely uneasy and counsels his daughter to "Look to my house," for last night he dreamt of money-bags, which he superstitiously construes as a bad omen.

Launcelot urges Shylock to go to the dinner. "My young master doth expect your reproach," he says (mistaking the word "reproach" for "approach"). Shylock answers, "So do I his," (meaning "reproach" in its true sense. Parodying Shylock's omen, Launcelot prophesies that there will be a masque, which does not please Shylock at all. He bids Jessica to shut up all the casements of the house when she hears the drum and the "wry-necked fife," and not to look upon "Christian fools with varnished faces." He tells her, "Let not the sound of shallow fopp'ry enter / My sober house." Launcelot leaves, whispering cryptically to Jessica to be on the lookout for a Christian "worth a Jew's eye," that is, Lorenzo. Shylock doesn't catch what he says but asks his daughter, "What says that fool of Hagar's offspring" (that is, outcast), and she replies that he merely had said farewell. Her father declares that Launcelot is kind enough but that he eats too much and sleeps by day, which makes him an unprofitable sort of servant. Shylock is glad that the clown will now help to waste Bassanio's money. Before he departs, Shylock sends Jessica inside and bids her lock the doors: "Fast bind, fast find—/ A proverb never stale in thrifty mind."

COMMENT AND SUMMARY. Shylock shows that his hatred has confused his thinking. In his first speech he warns Launcelot that he will get little to eat in Bassanio's house. A few moments later, he calls Bassanio a "prodigal Christian," that is, a spendthrift and waster. Indeed, Launcelot need not expect to "gormandize" in the house of a Christian gentleman who would value moderation in all things (as Portia does); at the same time, he may expect generous treatment, which is not the same thing as "wasteful." Shylock cannot understand the behavior of Christian gentlemen at all.

Launcelot, characteristically, provides more comedy in this scene at the expense of the Jew. First he echoes Shylock's call for Jessica, although he knows that his former master does not like him to act unbidden. (The echo carries on the comic theme of imitative servants, and Shylock's chiding suggests that Launcelot cannot learn the Jew's ways.) Then, when Shylock forecasts trouble, superstitiously interpreting his dream of moneybags as an ill-omen, Launcelot parodies his former master in a nonsensical interpretation of a nosebleed (believed to be a bad omen) as a prediction of a masque. He seems to misuse words consciously in this scene, puns wittily on the worth of a Christian, and generally demonstrates a change of character since his transference to Bassanio's service. Whereas in former scenes he plays a rustic clown, in this scene he appears to be a knowing fool whose superficial nonsense is really a cover for astute observation.

Shylock's character is augmented along the usual lines of the stereotyped Jew. Now we learn that, symbolically, Shylock thinks of his daughter in terms of money, for the ill omen is of her elopement as well as her theft, while the prophetic dream is only of money. This idea will be developed further on in the play and is designed to suggest that Jews do not have natural family ties, that they breed money, not children. His loss of Jessica will not be tragic in this play, and the loss of his money will provide for a comic portrait of the Jew foiled.

Shakespeare had a tendecy to portray his villains as puritanical types (see Prince John in *2 Henry IV* and Iago in *Othello*). Possibly he was objecting to the Puritan movement then rising in England. Shylock is no exception. He hates masques and music and regards the disguised or costumed Christians who participate in such activities as "fools with varnished faces." His objection to music is significant, in this entirely derogatory portrait of Shylock, for it signifies that his soul is damned. Speaking from the Christian point of view (Act V), Lorenzo later says, "That man that hath no music in himself, / Nor is not moved with concord of sweet sound, / Is fit for treasons, stratagems, and spoils; / The motions of his spirit are as dull as night, / And his affections dark as Erebus. / Let no such man be trusted." Shylock is just such a man.

Elements of Shylock's character, introduced earlier in the play, are also continued in this scene. He swears "By Jacob's staff," which Jacob had used to breed speckled ewes and rams, and which is a symbol of usury or interest to Shylock. He decides to "go in hate, to feed upon / The prodigal Christian," using a phrase which literally means "to dine at the expense of" but which has unpleasant connotations of "devour." He seems compelled to go "feasting" even when he has no mind to. Both these remarks suggest Shylock's carnality and cannibalism again. His miserliness is given added emphasis in Shylock's ironic parting words: "Fast bind, fast find—."

Jessica is seen briefly once more, this time at home in her "hell," which consists of locked doors and closed casements, sober silence within, while the world outside rejoices. Her deception of her father, already suggested, is demonstrated dramatically when she lies about Launcelot's message from Lorenzo.

Act Two, Scene Six

Gratiano and Salarino, disguised for the masque, are waiting for Lorenzo in front of Shylock's house. Gratiano marvels that Lorenzo is so late for a love rendezvous since lovers usually "run before the clock." But Salarino reflects that lovers hasten more when they make a promise than when they must keep it. Gratiano agrees, supporting his thought with the proverbial ideas that the man who sits down eagerly to a feast rises satiated; the horse that first races down a path returns wearily, and the ship that sets out gaily decked like a prodigal son returns again weather-beaten and "beggared by the strumpet wind." Cynically, Gratiano concludes, "All things that are / Are with more spirit chased than enjoyed."

At this moment, Lorenzo appears, apologizing for having been detained by business. He calls up to the window where Jessica appears, dressed in boy's clothing. She recognizes his voice but makes him identify himself anyway. He declares he is "Lorenzo and thy love," and she replies that he is her love, indeed, but is she his? Lorenzo reassures her. Jessica gives Lorenzo the casket she has stolen from her father and expresses embarrassment at being seen in boy's clothes. She objects to bearing Lorenzo's torch, for it will light her shames. Lorenzo assures her that no one will guess her true identity under her boy's disguise. When Jessica leaves the window to collect some more ducats, Gratiano praises her as "a gentile and no Jew," and Lorenzo swears he will love her in his "constant soul," for she is wise and fair and true. Jessica reappears on the street below, and they all exit.

COMMENT: The elopement of Jessica and Lorenzo is a typical device of romantic literature of the Renaissance. The nocturnal tryst, the presence of assisting friends, the wearing of disguises, are all or partly found in other Shakespearean plays (*Romeo and Juliet, Twelfth Night, Othello*). The nocturnal escape provides an appropriate romantic setting for the simple, lyrical, and beautiful love of Lorenzo and the lovely Jessica. Even Gratiano, who has just indulged in a string of cynical metaphors about lovers who are quick to surfeit, is so charmed by her aspect (appearances, again) that he refuses to accept her as a Jew and puns on her "gentile" nature.

Jessica's embarrassment at wearing boys' clothing was a comic twist in the Elizabethethan production of the play where all female parts were played by male actors. It was a stage convention derived from Italian comedy that the disguised individual is never detected by other characters in the play. Lorenzo's reassurance that Jessica's identity will remain well-hidden is a means of informing her and the audience of the fact. Since the discussion is relevant to a masque which is never held, it too appears to be a hangover from some earlier version of the play.

The romance of Lorenzo and Jessica operates as a parallel to the main action of the play, the romance of Bassanio and Portia. Jessica, like Portia, brings wealth to Lorenzo. Both ladies disguise as males; both are associated with caskets (Jessica gives a casket of stolen riches to Lorenzo and later Portia is won by the choosing of a casket); both ladies are "wise, fair, and true" and win the eternal love of their husbands in the "constant soul."

One of Jessica's endearing qualities is her sense of shame, suggesting both modesty and humility. She is ashamed of her "exchange," an ambiguous term which refers to her unnatural disguise as a boy and also to her unnatural behavior as a disloyal daughter. She is reluctant to hold up a candle to her "shames," a word which occurs in the plural and suggests that there is something besides the disguise that is troubling her. She finds that these shames "in themselves . . . are too too light," which is to say that her elopement, theft, and transvestism are improper, that deception comes too easily to her. At the same time, she paradoxically suggests that her shames are really an illumination, and that her entire life, actual and spiritual, will be (en)lightened by this shameful escape. For a better understanding of her dilemma, reread Launcelot's moral debate in II.ii where the clown is torn between obedience to the devil (Shylock) and to the fiend. By choosing to follow the "evil" counsel of the fiend, Launcelot actually improves his lot; by acting as a "shameful" daughter, Jessica is equally improved.

Antonio finds Gratiano and tells him that the masque has been called off, for the wind has changed and the voyagers must board the ship tonight. Gratiano says he is delighted to be able to leave at once.

SUMMARY. The scene is important for the following reasons:

1. The brief exchange of love pledges between Jessica and Lorenzo is hurried but convincing. Jessica is as charming as ever, modest about appearing in boys' attire and ashamed of having betrayed her father. These characterizations and the romantic subplot will be continued.

2. Gratiano's character as a gentleman fool is continued in his cynical reflections on the fickleness of lovers, which was a stock theme in the jests and jokes of the sixteenth century.

3. Preparation is made for a change of scene and action when Antonio announces that the masque has been called off because the wind has changed.

Act Two, Scene Seven

Back in Belmont, the Prince of Morocco is about to choose among the three caskets in the presence of Portia and others. The Prince looks over the inscriptions on each casket to determine which one contains Portia's picture. The lead casket reads, "Who chooseth me must give and hazard all he hath." This blunt warning does not appeal to the Prince, who will "hazard" for "fair advantages," not for mere lead. The inscription on the silver casket reads, "Who chooseth me shall get as much as he deserves." The Prince ponders this carefully: "weigh thy value with an even hand," he warns himself. "Rated" by his own "estimation," he deserves the lady by reason of his birth, breeding, fortune, and most of all by reason of the great love he bears her. Turning to the gold casket, however, he reads: "Who chooseth me shall gain what many men desire," and suddenly the puzzle seems very clear to him. What many men desire is the lady, for suitors undeterred by arduous voyages through the desert or over the ocean have come from all over the world to seek her. It would be sacrilege to put her picture in a lead or silver casket instead of a gold one. He recalls that in England there is a golden "coin" with the figure of an angel engraved on it. Here is an angel (Portia) lying on a golden bed (the casket). "Here I choose, and thrive I as I may."

Deciding to unlock the gold casket, the Prince is horrified to discover a picture of Death with a message written in his hollow eye: "All that glisters is not gold; / Often have you heard that told. / Many a man his life hath sold / But my outside to behold. / Gilded tombs do worms enfold." With a grieving heart the Prince takes a hasty leave of Portia, who is quite content to see the last of him, saying, "A gentle riddance . . . / Let all of his complexion choose me so."

COMMENT: The commercial talk of Venice is echoed in the Prince's speech. Terms like "hazard," "advantages," "value," "rated," "coin," and "thrive" suggest that Morocco thinks only of the material value of the caskets' metals and the advantages his choice might have to him. In his final decision, he is deceived by appearances.

The death's head with the message in its hollow eye is uncovered in its golden casket as a *memento mori*, a reminder of death, a favorite theme and image in sixteenth century European art and literature. The play reaches a moral apex in the disclosure of the message carried within the eye of the skull: "All that glisters is not gold . . ." This tense dramatic moment is well contrived to emphasize the theme of deceptive appearance, that there is a life beyond the one visible to man. The symbol of the death's head conveys a spiritual message to mankind, that the flesh dies while the soul lives forever. It is an exhortation to Christians to heed the dictates of their eternal souls which are too often subordinated to the demands of the flesh.

Morocco's association of the gold casket with an English coin called an "angel" and with the angelic Portia is a ludicrous and far-fetched piece of logic, intended to make the Prince appear ridiculous. Moreover, the Prince's eloquent language couched in hyperbole borders on bombast. The Prince is a caricature and is a portrayed as the Elizabethan stereotype of the Moor, a presumptuous and boastful warrior who is ignorant of European Christian values and of the distaste with which Europeans view his coloring.

Portia is relieved that Morocco has failed to chose correctly and bids "gentle riddance" (courteous and Christian riddance) to the Mohammedan Prince, punning on the word "gentile" as Antonio and Gratiano had done in connection with Shylock and Jessica, the main Jews in the play. Portia makes it abundantly clear that she personally does not favor a husband of dark "complexion" when she says, "Let all of his complexion choose me so." The ambiguous term "complexion" meant both "coloring" and "disposition," and the Moorish Prince is ill-favored in both.

SUMMARY. This scene is important for the following reasons:

1. The plot device of the caskets is implemented in this scene. We watch the Prince of Morocco as he deliberates over them, making himself ridiculous, and building tension as he ponders his choice.

2. We learn details of the legends on the caskets, and the content of the golden first choice—a death's head—is disclosed.

3. We learn that Portia is glad that the dark Prince chooses falsely and hopes that no other suitors of his color and disposition will try for her hand.

4. We are beginning to see the wisdom of the lottery, which was designed to weed out false lovers, whose faith in the appearance of things and blindness to inner values make two of them unacceptable as a husband to the worthy Portia.

Act Two, Scene Eight

In Venice once again, Salanio and Salarino are talking about recent events, particularly Shylock's reaction to the news that his daughter has run off with Lorenzo and has taken with her money and jewels of great value. Salarino explains that since Bassanio sailed for Belmont the same night that Lorenzo and Jessica eloped, Shylock suspected that the lovers were aboard the same ship. He brought the Duke of Venice down to the dock to search for them. But by the time they arrived it was too late, the ship was already gone. Furthermore, Antonio was there and swore that the lovers were not aboard, and the Duke learned from another source that Lorenzo and Jessica had been seen together in a gondola. Salarino is certain that Lorenzo is not on Bassanio's ship.

Salanio declares, "I never heard a passion so confused, / So strange, outrageous, and so variable / As the dog Jew did utter in the streets: / 'My daughter! O my ducats! O my daughter! / Fled with a Christian: . . . And jewels—two stones, two rich and precious stones, / Stol'n by my daughter! Justice! find the girl! / She hath the stones upon her. . . ." Salarino adds with enjoyment that all the boys of Venice now follow Shylock, "crying his stones, his daughter, and his ducats."

> **COMMENT:** Shylock is made to seem completely ridiculous. His reactions to Jessica's elopement and theft are described from the point of view of Salanio and Salarino, one of whom calls him "dog," and the other of whom paints the Jew as a grotesque and unnatural parent who cares more for his money than his daughter. They find him an appropriate object for Christian ridicule and enjoy the fact that the deceived usurer is bawdily mocked by the boys who cry "stones" (1. gems, 2. testicles) after him. Shylock's ominous dream of moneybags has come true, and the common prejudice that a Jew is only concerned with his money is given full expression in this scene.

In addition to the stereotype of the Jew, Shylock in this scene is said to behave like the "deceived father," a stock comic character in Renaissance comedy, whose protests against a daughter's elopement were often dramatized for the amusement of a conditioned audience. Shylock in this second-hand account is both deceived father and deceived Jew, another stock character of Italian street farce, rolled into one ridiculous creation designed to arouse the scornful daughter of the Elizabethan audience. What is remarkable about this caricature is that Shakespeare had it narrated and did not choose to dramatize it. This refusal to dramatize stock jokes may be taken as a sign of the extreme sensibility of the playwright to the human character he had created in Shylock.

Salanio recalls Antonio's debt next, and ominously remarks that Antonio will be made to pay for Shylock's loss if he does not meet his bond on time. To which Salarino adds that he had been thinking of Antonio's bond only yesterday, while listening to a report of a Venetian ship that had foundered in the English Channel; he had hoped it was not Antonio's ship.

COMMENT: This is another instance of foreshadowing, the anticipation of subsequent events in the play. Shylock's motive for revenge against Antonio later on is partly explained by the loss of his daughter and money at this point in the play. Such a motive is not just, but Shylock is in a "passion so confused," it should be remembered.

The two men agree to be gentle in breaking the news of the sunken Venetian vessel to Antonio, for "a kinder gentleman treads not the earth." As proof of Antonio's kindness and generosity, Salarino describes Antonio's parting from his friend Bassanio. Bassanio had promised to return as quickly as possible, but Antonio had urged him not to hurry for his sake and not to worry about the Jew's bond. Bassanio was to take all the time he needed in Belmont for the courtship and "fair ostents of love." Antonio had bidden his friend goodby with tears in his eyes, at which Salanio declares, "I think he only loves the world for him." The two gentlemen go off to seek Antonio to cheer him as best they can.

COMMENT AND SUMMARY. As a contrast to Shylock's "outrageous" and despicable behavior, labelled and described in the first half of this brief scene, Antonio's gentle, generous, and loyal character is described in the latter half with an accompanying anecdote proving his loyal friendship, which is a major theme in this play.

The juxtaposition of these two character sketches prepares the way for the confrontation of Antonio and Shylock, men of opposing natures and beliefs, in the famous trial scene of the play. The personality traits revealed here in the descriptive narratives will be dramatized and should be remembered at that point. The scene provides a caricature of Shylock and a character sketch of Antonio, in which the hate of one is opposed to the love of the other. The scene acts as a transition between events and serves to move the plot from one point to another, by relating details of the plot which are not dramatized. Suspense is created by the suggestion that one of Antonio's ships may be lost.

Act Two, Scene Nine

In Belmont once again, the Prince of Aragon has taken the oath and is coming to choose among the caskets. Nerissa draws the curtains that conceal the three caskets and, with a flourish of horns, Portia enters with the Prince. He promises never to reveal to anyone which casket he chose and, if he fails, never to woo another maid in marriage, and to leave Belmont immediately. Portia explains that all who seek her "worthless self" take the same oath.

Arragon, like Morocco, quickly passes over the lead casket, saying, "You shall look fairer ere I give or hazard." Then, turning to the gold casket, he reads the inscription: "Who chooseth me shall gain what many men desire." Here, pausing to consider what this may mean, he decides that the "many" are the fool multitude that choose by show, / Not learning more than the fond eye doth teach." He refers to the martlet, a bird that builds its nest on the outer walls of buildings and foolishly imagines itself safe from danger there. He, for his part, will not be deceived by outward appearances like the "barbarous multitudes."

Turning then to the silver casket, he reads: "Who chooseth me shall get as much as he deserves," which strikes him as just and proper, for no one should be granted privileges and titles of which he is unworthy. Pondering over the business at hand, the Prince muses that if all estates and offices were obtained purely on the basis of merit, there would be many reversals of fortune in the ranks of men. "How many then should cover [wear a hat] that stand bare, / How many be commanded that command."

Deciding to pick the silver casket on the basis of his own merit, the Prince unlocks the casket only to find inside the portrait of a blinking idot. "Did I deserve no more than a fool's head?" he laments: "Is that my prize? Are my deserts no better?" Portia explains that his error was in presuming to judge his own worth, which is only for others to do. Along with the picture of the idiot in the casket is a scroll, which reads in part, "Take what wife you will to bed, / I will ever be your head. So be gone; you are sped." The Prince exits with his followers, and Portia remarks that these fools think they are so smart when they choose, but in fact have only wit enough to lose; and Nerissa adds that the fate of man is not in his own hands: "Hanging and wiving go by destiny."

COMMENT: The choosing of the caskets by Arragon parallels but does not precisely duplicate the scene in which Morocco chooses. A number of details are added to those already known about the rules of the lottery—the unsuccessful lover may not reveal his choice, for example, and he must leave Portia and Belmont immediately. Since there are three secret messages enclosed in each casket, each scene of choosing brings with it the pleasure of disclosure. Note that the first two suitors are each princes of foreign powers and that neither of them are sound of judgment or worthy of marriage with Portia. A satirical barb is intended, no doubt, at the careless values of contemporary princes. Only a perfect Christian gentleman like Bassanio may have Portia, who displays her humility here by referring to herself as "my worthless self."

Arragon is unconsciously ironic when he refers to the "fool multitude that choose by show," for he will do the same. The "martlet" referred to is a foolish bird who builds its nest on the outer walls of buildings which only seem to be safe. The image of the martlet is associated elsewhere in Shakespeare with the theme of deceptive appearances (see Caroline Spurgeon's *Shakespeare's Imagery.*) Despite his awareness that appearances are often deceptive, Arragon is fooled by his own pride. He imagines himself more than a "common spirit" or the "barbarous multitudes" (with an unconscious allusion to Morocco). The proud Spanish Prince is unable to reason correctly because he is blinded by a false notion of his own desires into choosing the fool's casket. The moral comment on his choice is graphically illustrated by the portrait of a blinking idiot, a thorough fool, which he finds inside. The fool's head, like the death's head, was a significant and popular image in medieval and Renaissance satirical art. It symbolizes the folly of man who too often submitted to pride, the first of the deadly sins, forgetting that faith, not reason, is the only true wisdom for man.

A servant (whom Portia addresses as "my lord") enters to announce the arrival of a young Venetian, who precedes his lord with courteous messages and rich gifts. The servant, greatly impressed with the new arrival, says that he has never seen "So likely an ambassador of love. / A day in April never came so sweet / To show how costly summer was at hand, / As this fore-spurrer comes before his lord." Portia pretends to take the news lightly and teases the servant that the Venetian must be a relative of his since he praises him so lavishly, but Nerissa prays that the Venetian will turn out to be Bassanio.

COMMENT: Portia is evidently feeling light-hearted, for she playfully calls her servant "my lord." This servant has undoubtedly seen all the suitors who have come so far, but none has made the favorable impression that the Venetian envoy makes. The advance arrival must be Gratiano in his assumed refinement. We may be sure that Bassanio is not far behind. Notice that the servant has judged the suitor by the appearance of his ambassador and that he associates the visitor with true romance by describing him in terms of a sweet day in April.

SUMMARY. The scene is important for the following reasons:

1. The casket plot is advanced as the proud Prince of Arragon chooses the silver box and wins a fool's head as his prize.

2. The theme of deceptive appearances is sustained and enriched by the theme of foolish wisdom.

3. The correct choosing of the casket is prepared for by Portia's clue that the man with judgment of heart, not of wit, will win the prize, and by the servant's announcement of the arrival of a fair envoy (Gratiano).

Act Three, Scene One

Salanio and Salarino are discussing Antonio's affairs again. The news on the Rialto (the Venetian marketplace) is that Antonio has lost a rich ship on the Goodwin Sands in the English Channel. Salarino (comparing Report to an Elizabethan gossip who drinks ale and discusses her personal affairs among her cronies, pretending that she regrets the death of her third husband) hopes that Report is as much a liar as the tavern crone. Once more he praises "good Antonio," "honest Antonio," and wishes he had words more worthy of Antonio's name, but Salarino cuts short the eulogy and learns that Salanio is convinced that Antonio has lost a ship. Catching sight of Shylock at this moment, Salarino crosses himself to protect the prayer he has just made for Antonio, for he imagines that the devil incarnate comes "in the likeness of a Jew."

> **COMMENT:** Salarino's reference to "gossip Report" is important enough to warrant Salanio's extended development of her figure as an Elizabethan tavern crone. This homely conceit serves to emphasize the capricious and untrustworthy nature of Report (a personification of news both true and false, also called Rumour and Fame), for it will turn out later that Antonio's ships have not come to permanent harm at all and that the crone is a liar. The conceit of the crone provides us with a microcosmic view of contemporary Tudor life and recalls the type of female immortalized in Chaucer's Wife of Bath and in Skelton's Elinor Rummynge.
>
> Salarino's belief that the Jew was the devil incarnate was commonplace enough and is expressed earlier in the play by Launcelot Gobbo. It is a piece of comedy injected at this point to prepare for the arrival of Shylock.

Shylock enters, an catching sight of the two young men, accuses them of being involved in his daughter's elopement. Salarino readily admits that he knew of the plans, and Salanio declares that Shylock himself must have known that Jessica was likely to leave her "dam" (parent). Shylock swears that she is damned for it, but Salarino replies that she will be damned only if the devil (that is, Shylock) is her judge. Outraged at the thought of her disobedience, Shylock exclaims with indignation, "My own flesh and blood to rebel!" at which Salarino taunts him as if Shylock meant by this phrase that he had lustful wishes. Shylock explains that he means that his daughter is his own flesh and blood, but Salarino insists that there is an even greater difference between Shylock and Jessica than there is between jet and ivory or between red and white wine.

> **COMMENT:** Shylock is enraged at the men whom he suspects correctly of having abetted his daughter's elopement, but the two Christian gentlemen parry Shylock's charges with witty word-play and anti-Semitic allusions, which were always reliable for securing laughs. Shylock turns "dam" into "damn," playing on these words without any hesitation, but he is too hateful and ill-tempered to win any admiration for his skill with words.
>
> Whatever justifications are to found for Shylock's grievance over the elopement of Jessica, they are countered by Salanio's sensible explanation that it is the nature of children to leave their parents when they are old enough and ready to do so. Shylock must have known this, Salanio says. As for Jessica's fleshkinship to the usurer, Salanio claims that she is literally and figuratively vastly different in flesh from the old Jewish devil. She is a "white Jew," so to speak, and is associated with ivory and white (Rhenish) wine, while Shylock is associated with jet and red wine. (We may compare the white-and-black or red, (that is, the good-and-evil symbols, at this point, with similar ones used in connection with the Mohammedan Prince of Morocco, who was so proud of his dark complexion and red blood.) Christians or "gentle" people are characteristically associated with white; Jews, Mohammedans, and other villains and fools are associated with black and red.

Salarino asks Shylock for news of Antonio's ship, and the usurer replies that the merchant is surely bankrupt. He warns that Antonio had better "look to his bond," for Shylock intends to get even with him for the past. "He was wont to call me usurer," says Shylock; "He was wont to lend money for a Christian cursy" (courtesy), but now Shylock intends to get revenge for the past. Salarino declares he cannot believe that Shylock would take a pound of flesh, which is not good for anything, but the Jew insists that he has every intention of doing just that.

In a long and passionate speech, Shylock declares that he will use the flesh "to bait fish withal" if nothing else. In short, it will feed his revenge, for Antonio has disgraced him, hindered his business, laughed at his losses, mocked at his gains, scorned his nation, thwarted his bargains, cooled his friends, and heated his enemies. "And what's his reason? I am a Jew. Hath not a Jew eyes? Hath not a Jew hands, organs, dimensions, senses, affections, passions?—fed with the same food, hurt with the same weapons, subject to the same diseases, healed by the same means, warmed and cooled by the same winter and summer as a Christian is? If you prick us, do we not bleed? If you tickle us, do we not laugh? If you poison us, do we not die? And if you wrong us, shall we not revenge? If we are like you in the rest, we will resemble you in that."

COMMENT: This is one of the most interesting speeches in the play and one of the most problematical. Modern historical critics like E. E. Stoll and John Palmer support the view that Shakespeare's audience would have laughed at Shylock's assertion that the Jew is essentially no different from anyone else. Many Elizabethans believed as Launcelot and Salarino do, that the Jew was the devil incarnate. Everything that Shylock says in his famous explanation of his motives elicited the scorn of the Renaissance Christian, who believed that hatred and revenge were inherent Jewish traits.

The carnal or cannibalistic motiff is introduced at the start when Shylock says he will feed fish with Antonio's flesh or "feed my revenge." And Shylock's entire description of Jewish-Christian similarities is based strictly on fleshly resemblances. Both Jew and Christian have "hands, organs, dimensions, senses, affections, passions." They eat the same food, another carnal habit; they bleed in the same way, another manifestation of bodily or physical likeness. And so on. But there the resemblance ends.

In the flesh, Jew and Christian may be very much alike. In the spirit, in their ways and manners, they are entirely different. This is the whole point which Shylock (and the Romantic reader) misses, which our Christian playwright thought a Jew would miss, and which the Christian audience believed constituted the essential and irrefutable difference. Shylook is totally lacking in gentle (and gentile) ways. He repays humiliation with revenge, not Christian "humility" (charity). He hates his enemy whom Christians are taught to love; he does not understand the "quality of mercy," we hear later, or any of the precepts in the Sermon on the Mount, which was intepreted by Christians as an overthrow, rather than an outgrowth, of Judaic law. Anti-Semitism which began with *New Testament* charges against the Pharisees was embedded in the Christian mind. The Pharisees' literal adherence to the fleshly laws of the *Old Testament* and their ignorance of the spirit of the law were major concerns of Jesus himself. Antonio *does* hate Shylock because he is a Jew, and Shylock accurately answers his own question on this matter: "What's his reason? I am a Jew."

Shakespeare's applause need not be based on the false notion of his futuristic tolerance of members of different races and religions, as Romantic critics once felt. Ridiculous black Moroccans and devilish Jews made good theater in Shakespeare's day, and they were designed within the prejudiced frame of reference of Elizabethan times. What is meritorious in the creation of Shylock, who could be seen in no other way by the Renaissance man, is that every aspect of this devilish incarnation is explored, and a serious attempt, which goes far beyond conventional vice comedy, is made to explain his malicious *raison d'etre*.

Comic characterization in Shakespeare's day meant the creation of a figure who embodied the vices as Renaissance Christians knew them. But Shakespeare went a step further than other writers of his time. He probed into the nature of villainy itself. He mixed the comedy of vice with the examination of evil, a much more awesome thing, and achieved strangely mixed comic creations that are neither completely ridiculous nor totally terrifying, but have in them the power to move the pity of modern audiences whose moral values are much more flexible than were the Elizabethans'. Shakespeare's comic characterizations often have an ambiguity that is difficult to comprehend and invites thoughtful probing.

One of Antonio's servants comes seeking Salanio and Salarino, who leave with him just after Tubal, another Jew and Shylock's friend, arrives, but not before Salanio has associated Tubal also with the devil. Shylock eagerly asks his friend, who has just come from Genoa, whether he found Jessica there. Tubal answers that he often heard of her but was unable to find her. Shylock moans, "Why there, there, there, there! A diamond gone cost me two thousand ducats in Frankford! The curse never fell upon our nation till now; I never felt it till now. Two thousand ducats in that, and other precious, precious jewels. I would my daughter were dead at my foot, and the jewels in her ear! Would she were hearsed at my foot and the ducats in her coffin!"

COMMENT: Shakespeare makes it appear that Shylock's chief concern is the recovery of the money and jewels that his daughter has stolen. This would prove, indeed, that Shaylock was an unnatural and selfish man. Shylock's wish for Jessica's death may be a Christian interpretation of the Jewish tradition of preferring death to conversion, or to the custom of mourning as dead a Jewish man or woman who converts or marries a Christian, a custom which, in Elizabethan eyes would appear cruel or monstrous.

As if it were not enough to have Jessica steal his money, Shylock now bewails the loss of still more money spent in the search for her, "and no satisfaction, no revenge! Nor no ill luck stirring but what lights o' my shoulders, no sighs but o' my breathing, no tears but o' my shedding." Tubal reminds him that this is not really true. Antonio, for instance, has had a ship wrecked coming from Tripolis. Shylock pounces greedily on this news: "What, what, what? Ill luck, ill luck?", and then, "I thank God, I thank God! Is it true? Is it true?" Tubal assures him that he heard the news from one of the sailors in Genoa, and he adds that he also heard that Jessica spent eighty ducats in one night in Genoa. Miserable once more, Shylock exclaims: "Thou stick'st a dagger in me. I shall never see my gold again." Returning to the subject of Antonio. Tubal says that he met several of Antonio's creditors who are convinced that the merchant must be bankrupt. This information cheers Shylock again: "I am very glad of it. I'll plague him. I'll torture him. I am glad of it." Back to the subject of Jessica, Tubal remarks that he saw a ring that Jessica gave for a monkey, and Shylock, horrified, laments, "It was my turquoise; I had it of Leah when I was a bachelor. I would not have given it for a wilderness of monkeys." Tubal reminds him again that Antonio is certainly undone, and Shylock, determined to have vengeance, bids Tubal provide for an officer to arrest Antonio when the bond falls due. "I will have the heart of him if he forfeit, for were he out of Venice I can make what merchandise I will. Go, Tubal, and meet me at our synagogue; go, good Tubal; at our synogogue, Tubal."

COMMENT: Shylock is definitely a comic as well as sinister character in this scene. The theme of vengeance runs throughout his speeches, but he remains essentially comic because of his rapid shift in mood from despair to elation and back again, according to whether he thinks about his lost money or about Antonio's ill luck. As usual, Shylock repeats words and phrases over and over again, which adds to the comic effect.

SUMMARY. This scene is important for the following reasons:

1. We see the contemptuous way in which Salarino and Salanio treat Shylock, and we hear him tell them as well as Tubal of his absolute determination to have his bond from Antonio if his payment is late.

2. This scene contains the very famous speech by Shylock in which he insists that Jews are just as susceptible to physical suffering as Christians. Protesting Antonio's discrimination against him because of his religion, he says that Jews have learned from Christians how to seek revenge.

3. We learn that Antonio may have lost another ship. The plot thickens.

4. Tubal reports that Jessica is spending money freely in Genoa, and Shylock wishes his daughter dead with jewels and all upon her.

5. Once again Jessica's elopement is set beside Antonio's misfortunes, associating the two in Shylock's and our own minds. By association and not by direct statement, the motive for Shylock's cruelty toward Antonio is established as a desire to avenge the loss of his money and his daughter.

Act Three, Scene Two

In Belmont again, Bassanio is ready to choose among the caskets. Portia urges him to wait a day or two, for she fears to lose his company if he chooses incorrectly. Too modest to confess her love directly, she remarks, "There's something tell me, but it is not love, / I would not lose you; and you know yourself / Hate counsels not in such a quality." She wishes he could stay a month or two so she could teach him how to choose correctly, but then she would be breaking faith, and this she will not do. She tells him that his eyes have divided her in two: one half is his and the other half is also his, for what is hers is also his. Talking on at length, she is trying to draw out the time before he must choose, but Bassanio begs to be allowed to try his fortune, for he cannot bear the rack on which he lives. Portia teases Bassanio for his use of he word "rack," playfully accusing him of confessing love only in order to end his torture. Taking Portia's suggestion that he "confess and live," Bassanio answers that "confess and love" is all there is to admit. He is pleased that his torturer (Portia) "doth teach me answers for deliverance."

> **COMMENT:** Portia and Bassanio are obviously attuned to each other, for Bassanio quickly learns how to use Portia's hint for his "deliverance." The harmonious lovers speak the courteous and witty language of love, which is saturated with religious connotation and demonstrates the correspondence in thought between the noble love of man and woman and the higher love which is eternal. "Promise me life, and I'll confess the truth," for example, is perfectly suited to a courtly love or religious context.

Portia finally bids him choose which casket contains her picture, saying, "If you do love me, you will find me out." She tells the others to stand all apart and orders music to be played while he chooses, so that if he fails he will make a swanlike end, fading in music. If he should win, however, then the music will be like the triumphant flourish when a new king is crowned or like the sweet sounds that a dreaming bridegroom hears at daybreak. She compares Bassanio to the young Alcides (Hercules) of mythology, who rescued the Trojan virgin from a sea monster, and herself to the sacrificed virgin, for her life and happiness depend on him.

> **COMMENT:** Portia displays all the graces of the perfect lady. She prefers to use modest understatement rather than open declaration of her love, saying that her feelings are not the result of hate, and she is willing to instruct her suitor in the ways of courteous love. Her allusion to Alcides' rescue of the virgin shows the depth of her feeling for Bassanio and her fear of losing him.
>
> The music called for at this point supplies the lyrical background for the romantically tense moment which ensues. It also works as a symbol of Portia's love, which like music is a manifestation of universal harmony.

While Bassanio comments on the caskets to himself, a song is heard, which begins: "Tell me where is fancy bred, / Or in the heart or in the head? How begot, how nourished? / Reply, reply."

Looking at the caskets, Bassanio first comments to himself that outward appearance is not to be trusted to reveal the inner truth of anything. He will not be duped by ornament, which so often deceives men in all affairs of life. In legal matters and in religion a gracious or learned voice often conceals evil and corruption. "There is no vice so simple but assumes / Some mark of virtue on his outward parts," Bassanio reflects. As if with his sixth sense, Bassanio unwittingly guesses at the contents of the boxes: "Upon supposed fairness, often known / To be the dowry of a second head, / The skull that bred them, in the sepulcher." Bassanio therefore will not put his trust in "gaudy gold" or silver, the "common drudge" used for business transaction. Instead, he chooses "meager lead," which threatens rather than promises anything.

COMMENT: During the choosing interlude, Bassanio gives no evidence that he heeds the words of the song or that he relies on hints that may be given in the song. He is too busy examining his own heart in order to make the crucial decision. Nevertheless, the song poses a three-line question, each of which ends in a word rhyming with "lead." A hint is definitely given to Bassanio, but the question that is more to the point is, does Bassanio need it? Bassanio's reasoning shows how wise he is; he is aware that "a second head" and "the skull" may lie behind "supposed fairness." Thus, he follows his heart and decides to hazard all for the lady he loves. There is a fairy tale quality in the conclusion of the casket subplot in that the man whom the lady truly loves is also the one who is deserving of her. This romantic notion is a clear reflection of the paradoxical Renaissance notion that all is not fair that seems so and that outer appearances reflect the inner nature of man.

Portia, overjoyed at seeing that Bassanio has chosen correctly, remarks in an aside, "O love be moderate, allay thy ecstacy / In measure rain thy joy, scant this excess. / I feel too much thy blessing. Make it less / For fear I surfeit."

COMMENT: We may recall that in Act One, Scene Two, Portia and Nerissa were talking about the virtue of moderation in all things and the evil of excess. Even at this moment of great joy, Portia has not forgotten the value of moderation, although her happiness is now complete.

Opening the leaden casket, Bassanio joyfully discovers Portia's picture inside. Amazed at the likeness of the portrait to the original, he wonders with a lover's amazement how the artist could have made the eyes so mobile, the lips so sweet, the hair so like a golden spider's web to trap the hearts of men, without himself falling in love with the sitter. Yet beautiful though the picture is, Bassanio declares it is but a poor shadow of the living Portia.

COMMENT: Bassanio shows that among his other virtues he is a good judge of painting. Using the conventional language and imagery of sixteenth century love poetry, he praises the virtues of the picture, using the popular conceit of shadow and substance (underscoring the theme of appearance vs. reality), making a familiar analogy between the arts of painting and poetry, finding language insufficient to do justice to the portrait, and declaring both arts inferior to the living reality, Portia herself.

Together with the portrait is a congratulatory scroll that praises Bassanio for not choosing by external appearance, wishes him all good fortune, and bids him claim his lady with a loving kiss. Bassanio kisses Portia and remarks that he is still giddy with delight, unable quite to believe the reality of his good fortune.

Portia tells him that although for herself she would not be ambitious to be different, yet for his sake she wishes she were "A thousands time more fair, / Ten thousand times as rich," so that she might stand higher in his estimation and bring him greater delight. But, she confesses, the sum of herself "Is an unlessoned girl, unschooled, unpractised; / Happy in this, she is not yet so old / But she may learn; happier than this, / She is not bred so dull but she can learn; / Happiest of all, is that her gentle spirit / Commits itself to yours to be directed, / As from her lord, her governor, her king." She declares that everything she has is now his to command, in token of which she gives him a ring, bidding him guard it always as the symbol of their love. Bassanio swears that he will die rather than part with the ring.

> **COMMENT:** Portia's acceptance speech to her lord Bassanio displays her in the full flower of perfect Renaissance womanhood. She is not ambitious, that is, she is quiet rather than restive. She is modest in her self-estimation. Her generous spirit makes her wish she had more virtue, wealth, and friends to give her husband than she already has. She humbly describes herself as an "unlessoned girl, unschooled, unpracticed," by which she means not that she is ill-educated but that she is ignorant of the ways of married love. However, she has a sufficient supply of animal spirits to make a good wife; she is "not bred so dull but she can learn." The religious quality of her love is suggested by the theological terminology she uses to express it; she is most happy to commit her "gentle [gentile] spirit" to the direction of "her lord," to whom she is now "converted."
>
> Bassanio has already made a total commitment to Portia's love; Portia's speech now shows that her love is at least as great and as generous as his. An ideal marriage is about to take place, in which gentleness, courtesy, and love will reign. Castiglione could not have planned a better marriage in his *Book of the Courtier*. Portia's total submission to her husband is in keeping with the code of behavior developed for the gentlewoman of Queen Elizabeth's time; but the code did not expect her to curb her intelligence, wit, imagination, or initiative, and it was understood that great ladies were often equal to the tasks of men when the need for their greatness arose. Portia's defense of Antonio will constitute just such a need later in the play, and Porita will meet it.
>
> The ring that Porita gives Bassanio in this scene is symbolic of the virginity which she also offers him. Later in the play, the ring will become the subject of several witty but bawdy jests on the chastity of wives. In the meantime, we may note how earnestly Bassanio promises to keep the ring until death.

Nerissa and Gratiano now announce that they too wish to be married, and they receive the congratualations of the future Lord and his Lady of Belmont. Just as Gratiano is making a ribald pun on a wager over which couple will have the first son, Lorenzo and Jessica unexpectedly appear, together with Salarino.

COMMENT: The blossoming of love between Nerissa and Gratiano parallels the love story of Portia and Bassanio, and of Lorenzo and Jessica, who suddenly appear at this point. Gratiano's brief explanation of the details of their courtship is sufficient unto the day, for his nature is apish as we have seen, and he imitates Bassanio's every move. Bassanio's influence is a good one in that he has led Gratiano to marry a wife who has studied and who imitates Portia's gentle and courteous ways. The compounding of felicity with felicity in the marriage of friends to friends was a conventional occurrence in the romantic comedy of the period.

Bassanio welcomes his friends, checking with Portia that he does not overstep his bound in thus exerting his newly won rights as a host. Lorenzo explains that although he and Jessica had not intended to come to Belmont, they had met Salarino traveling in this direction, and he had prevailed upon them to change their course. Salarino confirms Lorenzo's story, adding that he had a reason for bringing them along. He delivers Bassanio's greeting from Antonio and a letter, which Bassanio reads immediately. In the meantime, Gratiano urges Nerissa to make Jessica welcome. (Gratiano's engagement has already made him somewhat courteous, for he realizes that Jessica must be feeling shy and awkward and needs urging to feel welcome. Once again he imitates Bassanio, who has just welcomed Lorenzo.) The dismay that overcomes Bassanio as he reads the letter from Antonio prompts Portia to beg her husband to tell her what is the matter, for as his wife, she must share his sorrow as well as his joy.

COMMENT: We see for ourselves that Shylock's suspicion that Lorenzo and Jessica have escaped with Bassanio was totally unfounded, and that Antonio told the truth when he denied knowledge of their whereabouts. (A gentleman may equivocate, but he never lies.)

"Here are a few of the unpleasant'st words / That ever blotted paper," exclaims Bassanio. He explains to Portia that when he told her he was a gentleman with no money, / he was telling the truth, but he had omitted one very important fact, that a very dear friend of his bound himself to his keenest enemy to enable Bassanio to come to Belmont. Is it true, Bassanio asks Salarino, that all Antonio's ships have foundered at sea?

Salarino confirms the truth of the letter and adds that even if Antonio now had the money, Shylock would refuse it. Salarino declares that he never saw a creature so "greedy" to destroy his fellow man. Twenty merchants and the Duke have argued with him but no one can persuade him to relinquish his claim. Shylock threatens the Duke that if the bond is not held valid in court, foreigners will no longer trust in the justice of Venetian courts to uphold the legality of contracts. Jessica adds that when she was with him she had heard Shylock tell his friends "That he would rather have Antonio's flesh / Than twenty times the value of the sum / That he did owe him."

COMMENT: We learn that Bassanio had equivocated when he told Portia that "only my blood speaks to you in my veins," that his only wealth was the noble blood in his veins. Equivocation was an acceptable part of courtly behavior; it showed the linguistic skill of the gentleman who used it, and protected the gentleman from the necessity of being discourteous or of lying outright. Bassanio's grief is felt for Antonio, not for his omissions of truth during his courtship of Portia. His passionate self-recrimination is couched in the metaphorical language of flesh and blood (usually associated with Shylock), which Bassanio suddenly begins to use. He had used his friend to "feed my means"; the letter-paper is his friend's "body," and every word "a gaping wound / Issuing lifeblood." Through the use of this language, Bassanio reveals that he feels like an unnatural villain (like Shylock) because he has murdered his dearest friend.

The account Salarino gives of Shylock in connection with Antonio's forfeit continues the portrayal of the usurer as an unnatural and cannibalistic creature. Shylock bears the shape of man, which is to say, he appears to be a man, but the appearance is deceptive. He is "greedy" for Antonio's destruction. Jessica helps color the portrait by adding that Shylock had spoken in her hearing of his desire for "Antonio's flesh."

Bassanio explains to Portia that Antonio is not only his dear friend but also the kindest and best-natured man in Italy. When Portia learns that the sum of money in question is three thousand ducate, she exclaims: "What, no more? / Pay him six thousand, and deface the bond. / Double six thousand and then treble that, / Before a friend of this discription / Shall lose a hair through Bassanio's fault." She bids him come to church to be married immediately, and then he can haste away to Venice, "For never shall you lie by Portia's side / With an unquiet soul." After he has paid the debt, twenty times over if necessary, she bids him bring Antonio back with him to Belmont. In the meantime she and Nerissa will live like maidens or widows, awaiting the return of their husbands.

Bassanio reads aloud the letter from his friend, in which Antonio explains that all his ships have been lost and that his bond is forfeit. Antonio is resigned to the fact that in paying his debt to the Jew he must lose his life, and he absolves Bassanio of anything he owes him. His only wish in life now is to see Bassanio once more, but he tells his friend that he must do just as he pleases about coming to Venice. "If your love do not persuade you to come, let not my letter," Portia, deeply moved by these words, urges great haste, and Bassanio promises to hurry to and from Venice as quickly as possible.

COMMENT: Portia's generosity is put to the test sooner than either she or Bassanio could have expected, and her word is no more than her deed. With splendid munificence she offers him twenty times the "petty debt" to rescue his dear friend. We will shortly see that Portia has wit as well as money to contribute to Antonio's cause.

The letter from Antonio is brief and very touching. He utters not a single word of complaint about his predicament and lays no blame on Bassanio. The melancholy disposition of noble Antonio will stand him in good stead, for it permits him to face death with courage and resignation.

SUMMARY. This scene is interesting and significant for the following reasons:

1. We see that Portia loves Bassanio as he loves her and fervently hopes that he will choose the right casket, which he does. The device of the caskets proves to have been a wise invention of her father, in determining the perfect husband for his daughter.

2. Portia and Bassanio are overcome with happiness, and Portia wishes only that she had more to give her husband in the way of material and spiritual advantages. Bassanio, however, can hardly wish for more than this gracious and delightful woman.

3. Portia gives Bassanio a ring, bidding him to guard it closely as a token of her love for him and his for her. We will see later in the play the erotic conversation that arises in connection with this ring.

4. Nerissa and Gratiano announce that they plan to marry also. This news compounds the happiness of the moment and shows how inferiors may benefit by the influence of noble friends.

5. Salarino, accompanied by Lorenzo and Jessica, bring Bassanio the evil news that Shylock intends to claim the pound of flesh from Antonio, whose ships have all failed to return. Bassanio is deeply distressed, and explains the situation to Portia, who promplty agrees to supply whatever sum of money is necessary to save her husband's friend. The couples go off to be married before Baassanio and Gratiano depart for Venice.

Act Three, Scene Three

Antonio, guarded by the jailor and accompanied by Salanio, tries to speak to Shylock, but the usurer will not listen to his plea. Warning the jailer to keep a close watch on his charge, Shylock declares, "This is the fool that lent out money gratis." Antonio used to call him dog; well, now let him beware the fangs. "I'll not be made soft and dull-eyed fool, / To shake the head, relent, and sigh and yield / To Christian intercessors."

Antonio realizes there is no use in arguing or pleading any more with Shylock, who is bent on retaliating for all the times that Antonio saved other debtors from Sylock's extortions by lending them money free of interest. When Salanio tries to cheer the merchant by assuring him that the Duke will support him in court, Antonio does not respond. He believes that the Duke will be afraid of losing the confidence of the commercial community if he abrogates this one contract. Worn out by his griefs and losses, Antonio is resigned to his fate, and only hopes that

Bassanio will arrive from Belmont in time to see him pay his debt," and then I care not."

COMMENT AND SUMMARY. This brief scene juxtaposes the protogonist and antagonist, Antonio and Shylock, still another time. Their characters as usual are set up as a contrast. The exacting and merciless Shylock insists he will have his bond, and we learn that the generous Antonio has often saved other debtors from falling into Shylock's clutches.

The scene is incremental rather than repetitive, for while it repeats old emphases, it adds new facts to the characterizations. Shylock's unflinching cruelty is established by his refusal to listen to Antonio's plea. The dog-epithet is repeated over and over again by Shylock himself, and Shylock comically admits the horrible fact that he intends to behave like a dog, "since I am a dog." The humor of Shylock's self-characterization, however, escapes Salanio, who tags Shylock an "impenetrable cur," suggesting that his evil is dark and profound.

Antonio appears for the first time since his disaster in the role of suppliant to the usurer. We have already been prepared in the preceding scene to witness his grief and weariness. The present scene dramatizes Antonio as a melancholy man prepared to face death with courage and resignation.

Act Three, Scene Four

In Belmont once again Lorenzo tells Portia how much he admires her noble conception of love and the dignity with which she bears the absence of Bassanio. He assures her that if she knew all the virtues of Antonio, what a true gentleman and friend he is, she would be even more glad of helping him than of her usual acts of kindness.

Portia replies, "I never did repent for doing good, / Nor shall not now." She declares that since close friends are generally similar in proportion, lineaments, manners, and spirit, Antonio must resemble Bassanio, who in turn is the reflection of her own soul. Therefore no effort can be too great to rescue such a man from "hellish cruelty." Suddenly embarrassed by this talk which, she says "comes too near the praising of myself," she changes the subject.

COMMENT: Lorenzo recognizes quite rightly that Portia is an extraordinary person. Few women could so magnanimously part with their husbands on their wedding day and bear with such equanimity the absence of a beloved. Portia's generosity is enhanced by her modesty, and we will soon see that these noble qualities are equalled only by her resourceful wit.

Portia tells Lorenzo that she and Nerissa have decided to remain in a neighboring monastery to live in prayer and contemplation while their husbands are away. She asks Lorenzo and Jessica to act as master and mistress of her estate during her absence, and Lorenzo readily agrees. Jessica wishes Portia "all heart's content," and Portia returns the wish.

When Lorenzo and Jessica exit, Portia asks her servant (named Balthasar) to take a message to her cousin, Doctor Bellario in Padua, from whom he will receive certain papers and clothing. She bids him bring these as quickly as possible to the ferry that goes to Venice, where she will be waiting for him. The servant hurries away and Portia tells Nerissa that they will shortly see their husbands without being recognized, for the women will be dressed up as young men. The lady gaily bets her maid that when they are disguished she will be "the prettier fellow of the two." In her imagaination she looks forward to wearing her dagger with a brave grace; to speaking in a high piping voice midway between that of man and boy; to walking with a manly stride; and to bragging of all the women who have died of love for him (her). "I have within my mind / A thousand raw tricks of these bragging jacks / Which I will practice." Nerissa asks if they "'will turn to men," and Portia chides her maid for putting a lewd cast on her intentions. The coach is waiting for them, and Portia promises to explain her plan to Nerissa on the way.

COMMENT AND SUMMARY. We witness an exchange of courtesies between Portia and Lorenzo which shows us just how gentle people behave. The gracious manners and language exchanged between Porita and Lorenzo should be noted and contrasted with the conversations Shylock holds with his servant, daughter, friend, or with Christians. The one is filled with compliments and good wishes, the other is filled with expletive and ugly metaphor. The gentle people of the play speak of love, friendship and generosity; the Jew of the play discusses money, revenge, hatred, and flesh.

Portia expresses one of the notions of Renaissance idealism when she says that there are similarities in size, shape, and physical characteristics, as well as in manners and spirit, among deeply devoted friends and lovers. She reasons that since Antonio and Bassanio are such close friends, and since she and Bassanio are such close lovers, then Antonio must be a "semblance of my soul." Although her explanation of her generosity comes very close to self-praise, Portia is actually explicating the *New Testament* commandment, "Thou shalt love thy neighbour as thyself" (Matthew 22:29, but also see Leviticus 19:18). In addition, Portia describes Antonio's situation as a "state of hellish cruelty," suggesting once more that Shylock is really a demonic creature.

We learn that Portia intends to go to Venice in disguise, accompanied by Nerissa. Unlike Jessica (II.vi), Portia is not embarrassed by wearing boys' clothing. On the contrary, she plans to get into the spirit of the disguise, and describes the silly foibles of bragging youths, which she plans to imitate, and shows once more what an observant caricaturist she is.

Despite the serious nature of the journey she is undertaking, Portia is filled with high spirits over the coming adventure. When Nerissa consciously or otherwise uses the ambiguous term "turn to" (1. become, 2. seek sexually), Portia understands it in its lewd sense. She displays the eroticism of a young bride, but her sexual conversation, as we shall see, is delicate and indirect. It is the less gentle Nerissa who appears to give the lewd cast to her words.

Act Three, Scene Five

Jessica and Launcelot are talking together in Belmont some time after Portia has departed from the house. The clown tells the girl that he fears she is damned, for the Bible says that the sins of the father are laid upon the children, and she is daughter to the faithless Jew. He says that he can only think of "a kind of bastard hope" that may save her, the hope that Shylock did not beget her. Jessica replies that then "the sins of my mother should be visited upon me." Launcelet hadn't thought of that; he declares that here can be no hope for her salvation, but Jessica reminds him that she will be saved by her husband, who has made her a Christian. Launcelot is not pleased with this solution, insisting that there are enough Christians already without adding more converts who will eat pork and raise the price of hogs.

COMMENT: Launcelot has come to Belmont with Bassanio and has been left behind when his master returns to Venice. As in his earlier scene, he is preoccupied with the subject of illegitimacy and salvation. His jests turn on the hope that Jessica may be her mother's bastard and thereby avoid damnation for the faithlessness of her father. The clown's comic treatment of bastardy and salvation is a thin and ammusing disgiuse for the important theme of conversion which runs through this play. The conversion of Jews was a major concern among Christians, dating from the first century A. D. when the *New Testament* was written, and the conversion of Jessica is the crux of this scene.

At this moment Lorenzo appears and jestingly tells Launcelot that he will grow jealous of him if he gets Jessica into corners, but when his wife explains the nature of their conversation Lorenzo declares that he can answer the charge of raising the price of pork by converting Jessica to Christianity better than Launcelot can answer the charge of getting "the Moor" pregnant. Launcelot does not dispute this charge, merely playing on the words of his sentence: "It is *much* that the *Moor* should be more than reason; but if she be less than an honest woman, she is indeed *more* than I took her for."

COMMENT: Lorenzo's reference to "the Moor" it taken as evidence that Shakespeare, in writing *The Merchant,* had reworked an earlier play and had forgotten to tie up all the loose ends. However irrelevant this reference to the Moor may be, as the play stands, it teaches us that Moors and Negroes were regarded as the same, and that the "commonwealth" would look more harshly upon Launcelot's liaison with a Negro and the illegitimate child he had begotten upon her, than it would on Lorenzo's conversion of and marriage to a Jew. In the social hierarchy of the Renaissance Christian world we see, Jews were just a rung above Moors, and both were outcasts from the "commonweal."

Lorenzo throws up his hands at this nonsense, declaring that silence is better than such wit. He bids Launcelot tell the other servants to "prepare for dinner," and Launcelot replies, again with double meaning, that the servants are already prepared for dinner because they all have "stomachs" (sexual as well as eating appetites). He also refuses to "cover" (1. lay the tablecloth, 2. don a hat, 3. mount and impregnate the female), because he knows his duty. There is more punning by Launcelot on Lorenzo's order to "go to thy fellows, bid them cover the table, serve in the meat, and we will come in to dinner." Launcelot twists the words around so that they can be interpreted lewdly, and answers: "For the table, sir, it shall be served in; for the meat, sir, it sall be covered; for your coming in to dinner, sir, why let it be as humors and conceits shall govern."

Launcelot exits, and Lorenzo and Jessica remain on stage. Lorenzo comments that the clown's words show that he has a good memory, even if he makes utter nonsense of his wit. There are many fools "garnish'd like him" in higher social positions who, for the sake of "a tricky word," will obscure the sense of their matter.

COMMENT: The low-comedy of Launcelot is full of coarse sexual reference, calculated to amuse the "groundlings" (members of the lower class who paid a penny for standing room in the pit or orchestra), who probably came to see their favorite clown, Will Kemp, play the role. Launcelot's "wit-snapping" may be contrasted with the sexual allusions moderately sprinkled through the speeches of the romantic characters of the play. Launcelot's cruder double-entendres are intemperately heaped all in one place, exasperating Lorenzo, who is forced to ask, "Wilt thou show the whole wealth of thy wit in an instant?"

We have already seen that Lorenzo is a quiet man; now we learn that he is also a "plain man" who speaks with "plain meaning." Nevertheless, he tolerates the clown and appreciates his good memory and vocabulary inasmuch as fools in higher places willingly distort their meanings for the sake of an ambiguously clever word. Lorenzo is objecting to garnished speaking and false wit, which precious Elizabethans affected as a show of eloquence.

Lorenzo now asks his wife what she thinks of Portia, and Jessica replies that she cannot speak too highly of the lady of Belmont. She declares that Bassanio cannot help but live an upright life, "for, having such a blessing in his lady, / He finds the joys of heaven here on earth;" and if he does not deserve it here on earth, he is not likely to get it in heaven. As for Portia, "the poor rude world / Hath not her fellow."

COMMENT: In spite of her cloisetered life in a Jewish household, Jessica is instinctively aware of Christian values. She describes Portia in the very terms used in the neo-Platonic schools of the Renaissance, without having been raised in their tradition. Portia is a perfect lady of virtue through whose love the gentleman learns to live the blessed and upright life, which will assure his mortal and eternal joy, Jessica says. It is to be understood that Jessica has come to this way of thinking "in reason," or that Lorenzo has already schooled her in these ideas.

Lorenzo happily remarks that he is just such a husband to Jessica as Portia is wife to Bassanio, but Jessica pertly replies that he must ask her opinion on that matter. When Lorenzo suggests that they go in to dinner, Jessica observes that she had better praise him "while I have a stomach" (the pun here is on her 1. appetite, 2. inclination.) Lorenzo answers this with another pun, saying she had better leave the subject for table talk, and then he will digest her words along with the food, no matter how bad. Finally, Jessica adds the last witty word, "Well, I'll set you forth" (1. lay out a feast, 2. praise you highly).

COMMENT: When Lorenzo compares himself to Portia, saying "even such a husband / Hast thou of me," he is being playful. But at the same time, he indicates that as a Christian, he too will provide Jessica with the blessed life on earth and in heaven.

The romantic couple are infected by Launcelot's wit and pun on the same words as did the clown. The cheerful banter of the newly-wed couple is designed to show how courteous and how happy they are and how well they deserve the rewards Antonio will soon win for them.

SUMMARY. This scene is a carefree interlude in the midst of the serious concern about Antonio's welfare, but under the guise of levity it resolves several important questions about courtesy and salvation.

1. Launcelot's crude concern over Jessica's salvation reflects questions in the audience's mind, which are answered by Lorenzo's assurance that Jessica's conversion will do the trick.

2. Jessica portrays Portia as a perfect Christian lady, revealing as she does so that she herself is one too.

3. Launcelot provides coarse jests on the Elizabethan stereotype of the Moor and on the sexual appetites of servants, while in contrast Lorenzo and Jessica exchange courteous banter on more pleasant subjects.

Act Four, Scene One

The scene is the court in Venice, where the Duke is presiding over the case of Shylock's claim to his pound of flesh. Antonio, Bassanio, Gratiano, and other Venetian noblemen are already present. The Duke expresses his pity for Antonio, whose adversary he declares is "an inhuman wretch, / Uncapable of pity, void and empty / From any dram of mercy." Antonio replies that he knows that the Duke has done his utmost to persuade Shylock to be merciful but to no avail. The merchant realizes that the law holds him responsible for the bond, and he is prepared to bear with patience and a quiet spirit the brunt of Shylock's fury.

> **COMMENT:** In this famous courtroom scene, many threads of theme and character which run through the play are tied together. Antonio gives full expression to the characteristics of the melancholy Christian gentleman, which we have seen in part and of which we have been frequently told. The characters of Shylock and Antonio have been repeatedly set in opposition in earlier scenes, and once more are so placed by Antonio himself: "I do oppose / My patience to his fury." Antonio's Christian virtues are stated and displayed in his willingness "to suffer with a quietness of spirit" the tyranny of the Jew.

Shylock enters the court and stands before the Duke, who tries once more to soften his heart by telling the creditor that all those present think that he is merely pretending to be cruel until the moment of execution when he will, in fact, show mercy to his victim. The Duke declares that even Turks and Tartars, people known for their savagery and never trained in "tender courtesy," would show greater humanity towards a man such as Antonio who has suffered so many losses all at once. He tells the usurer, "We all expect a gentle answer, Jew," (punning on "gentile" again), but Shylock is unmoved by this as by all other appeals to "human gentleness and love." He declares that he was sworn "by our holy Sabbath" to have his bond, and he warns the Duke of the consequence for Venice if the law is not impartially observed in this as in all cases.

> **COMMENT:** The Duke's plea for "human gentleness and love" is symbolically a plea for the Jew's conversion. In the courtroom, the Duke expects Shylock to behave like a Christian, with "tender courtesy," and to give "gentle" (gentle, gentile) answers. Shylock, however, is obdurate, and as the Jewish moneylender of the play, he is symbolic of all Jews. When the Duke points out that, while the act of demanding the bond is a legal one, the thought or motive behind Shylock's demand is "malicious," he is engaging in the age-old controversy between *Old* and *New Testament* interpretations of the law of God. The Duke believes that Jews study and live by the letter of the old law, while Christians, he knows, live by the spirit of the old law, which is interpreted in the new. Metaphorically the old law was a "carnal commandment" (Hebrews 7:16), expressing "fleshly wisdom" rather than "the spirit of the living God" (2

Corinthians 3:3), and Shylock is its fleshly embodiment. Throughout the scene, Shylock's religious thought and practice are presented from the Christian point of view as literal, merciless, irrational, and heinously inhuman. Shylock's oath, "by our Holy Sabbath," is given as an example of how Jews desecreate the house of God by swearing in the temple (Matthew 5:33-37).

As for why Shylock prefers to have "the weight of carrion flesh" rather than his money, he announces quite simply that it is his "humor" (a physiological and mental disposition) to do so. He compares himself to man whose house is troubled by a rat and who is willing to pay ten thousand ducats to have it poisoned, which it is his privelege to do. "Some men there are love not a gaping pig, / Some that are mad if they behold a cat, / And others, when the bagpipe sings i' the nose, / Cannot contain their urine for affection, / Master of passion, sways it to the mood / Of what it likes or loathes." And just as there is no rational explanation of why one man hates a pig, why another cannot abide a harmless cat, and why a third cannot contain his urine when listening to a bagpipe, so Shylock cannot and will not give a reason for his action other than the deep-seated hatred and loathing that he bears Antonio.

COMMENT: Shylock's reasons for preferring the pound of flesh to money were confirmations of the stereotype so carefully built up in earlier scenes, and were a source of pleasure to the sanguine audience of Shakespeare's time. When Shylock says it is his "humor" to prefer flesh to money, he is proving a Christian point that Jews lived by "carnal commandments," that they really were unnatural creatures. Shylock implies that his desire for Antonio's flesh is no more than an affection and is completely inexplicable; he can "give no reason," nor will he. Earlier in the play we have heard him justify his hatred of Antonio as the natural desire for revenge against a man who has injured his business prospects and his self-esteem in the past. We have heard Shylock say that if Antonio were gone from the community the usury business would improve, and we have heard him express hatred for the Christian Venetians in general for making him an outcast from society and especially for stealing his daughter and much of his money away from him. But here in court, Shylock mentions none of these reasons. Instead, he makes himself ridiculous by comparing the unreasoning hatred he feels for Antonio with the irrational and inexplicable impulses found in all men. The examples that he gives of human nature mastered by strange and powerful passions are such as to excite disgust and contempt in his hearers. Yet Shylock seems to find them natural and unavoidable. The man who is overcome with loathing for a pig or cat, or a man who cannot contain his urine when he hears the bagpipe playing, are ridiculous types, and Shylock, by analogy, is ridiculous too. Shylock, however, is unaware of this and seems to embrace the ridiculous and the inexplicable in human nature as justification for his own passionate hatred of Antonio, which has now reached the point of murder.

> From the Christian point of view, Shylock the Jew represents evil, the devil, anti-Christ, and all the forces of disorder, for he is unable to understand the Christian sense of right and wrong, which controls the behavior of the others in the courtroom.

Bassanio heatedly objects that Shylock has given no excuse for his cruelty, for all men do not kill that which they do not love, but the Jew replies that he is not bound to please Bassanio by his answers. He declares that no man truly hates that which he would not kill, and, having once been stung by a serpent (Antonio), he will not give it a chance to sting him again.

Antonio begs Bassanio not to argue with his creditor. "You may as well go stand upon the beach / And bid the main flood bate his usual height; / You may as well use question with the wolf, / Why he hath made the ewe bleat for the lamb. / You may as well forbid the mountain pines / To wag their high tops and to make no noise / When they are fretten with the gusts of heaven," as to seek to soften that hardest of all things, Shylock's "Jewish heart." Accepting his plight, Antonio asks that the court proceed to render judgment, but Bassanio makes one last attempt, offering Shylock six thousand ducats instead of the original three thousand. Shylock, implacable, replies that if he were offered six times the original sum he would not take it but would insist upon his bond.

> **COMMENT:** Of all present, Bassanio is by far the man most troubled by Antonio's plight, for he keenly feels his personal responsibility for the bond which his friend signed for his sake. Therefore, though Antonio is stoically resigned to his fate, Bassanio is not yet ready to give up the attempt to try to persuade Shylock to spare the merchant.
>
> It is Antonio, however, and not Bassanio, who understands the nature of their adversary. Earlier in the scene, the Duke called Shylock an "inhuman wretch," and that is exactly what Shylock shows he is, inhuman. What distinguishes a man from the animal world is the fact that man can be swayed by the voice of reason and of compassion. As Antonio remarks, however, Shylock's impulses to vengeance is as powerful and as elemental as any force of nature. Man can have as little hope to move him as to move the fierce wolf or the towering pine.

Intervening once more, the Duke asks Shylock how he can hope for mercy for himself when he shows none to others, but Shylock simply replies: "What judgment shall I dread, doing no wrong?" He tells his listeners that just as they have purchased slaves whom they treat like dogs or beasts of burden, so he is master of Antonio, whom he has bought with his money. And just as the Venetian nobles would never agree to free their slaves, so Shylock declares he will not set Antonio free, but will dispose of him as he pleases. He asks for justice and reminds the Duke that the prosperity of Venice will suffer if the law is not maintained in the city.

COMMENT: The Duke uses the Christian argument for mercy (Matthew 5:7), but Shylock refuses to admit that he is doing anything wrong, for according to his scrupulously legalistic and allegedly Jewish way of looking at the world, wrongdoing consists merely in breaking the letter of the law. Since by taking Antonio's flesh he will be fulfilling the terms of a legal contract, Shylock insists that his action is right, for it is lawful. He ignores, as it is the nature of the stereotyped Jew to do, the spirit of the law, which requires mercy to one's fellow man and even to one's enemy.

From the modern's point of view, Shylock's comparison between his hold over Antonio and the power exercised by these self-righteous Venetian noblemen over their slaves, is the most effective justification he has offered for his conduct. What right do these slave-holders have to condemn him for disposing as he pleases with his human property as they do with theirs? No one present answers this challenge, and the silence on this subject raises a moot question about Shakespeare's attitude toward slaves.

It has been abundantly clear in the play, however, that servants in the homes of Christians were well treated and that they learned, by imitation of their masters, to behave in gentle ways. The Christian gentleman set a good example for his servant and thus guided the unwise and the untutored into the right way of life. Christians would not agree with Shylock that they abused their slaves, and Shylock has been wrong before about the treatment Launcelot would get in a gentile's service. Shylock himself does not believe in freeing slaves; he simply brings up the subject because they, like Antonio's flesh, are human possessions. The analogy was ridiculous to Renaissance Christians, who would never compare a Christian gentleman to an ignoble slave. The gentleman was born to command, the slave to follow. (Relevant to this issue is the historical fact that medieval Jews were forbidden to keep Christian slaves. Pagan slaves in the service of Jews were given their freedom upon conversion to Christianity.)

The Duke declares that he may dismiss the court unless Bellario, the learned jurist from Padua, arrives to determine the case. Salarino then announces that a messenger from Bellario is waiting outside. While this messenger is being sent for, Bassanio tries to cheer Antonio, swearing that he would rather die than permit Antonio to lose one drop of blood. Antonio, however, protests that he is more ready and more fit for death than his friend: "I am a tainted wether of the flock, / Meetest for death."

COMMENT: With characteristic melancholy, Antonio compares himself to a "wether" (a castrated male sheep) and to the "weakest kind of fruit," which are more fit to die than Bassanio, who, it is implied, is young, strong, virile, and high-spirited, who enjoys life and, therefore, should be allowed to live it. Antonio confirms what has already been implied, that he is an older man, no longer suited for the dance of love, that he has entered the contemplative stage of life and is ready for death.

Nerissa enters dressed as a lawyer's clerk, and while the Duke reads the letters that she brings from Bellario, Bassanio anxiously watches Shylock whetting his knife for the operation. Gratiano cannot contain himself at this sight. He declares that Shylock sharpenes the knife on his very *soul* rather than on the *sole* of his foot, for no metal is as keen as the villain's sharp envy. Gratiano is almost ready to believe with Pythagoras that the souls of dead animals enter the bodies of men, since no other theory can explain Shylock's currish spirit, so "wolvish, bloody, starved, and ravenous." (Pythagoras was an ancient Greek philosopher who believed in the transmigration of souls after death.) Shylock, however, calmly replies to Gratiano that all his anger and harsh words cannot alter the seal upon the lawful bond. "I stand here for law," Shylock asserts.

Having read the letter, the Duke sends Nerissa to fetch Portia, and while she is gone he reads aloud the message from old Bellario, who explains that although he is too sick to come, he is sending in his stead a young and learned doctor of jurisprudence named Balthasar. He begs the Duke not to be apprehensive on account of the lawyer's extreme youth, promising that this Balthasar will bring to bear on the case both Bellario's considered opinion and his own learned judgment.

COMMENT: The interlude between Gratiano and Shylock augments the characterization of Shylock as an unnatural dog and of Gratiano as a loyal but coarse friend. Shylock's last statement, "I stand here for the law," not only is relevant in the context of the play, but signifies that Shylock represents the literal interpretation of *Old Testament* law. Portia's famous mercy-speech, which follows shortly, is set in direct opposition to Shylock's courtroom literalness.

Portia's disguise as a doctor is a dramatic necessity at this point in the play, for she could not plead in court as a woman, nor could a male doctor (say, Bassanio) have pleaded so convincingly for mercy, which was commonly regarded as a womanly virtue and one which men learned from women.

Portia enters, dressed as a Doctor of Law, and is welcomed by the Duke. Bidding the merchant and the Jew stand forth, she hears Antonio confess that he has signed the bond in question, and she declares, "Then must the Jew be merciful." When Shylock demands to know on what grounds he must be merciful, the young lawyer replies: "The quality of mercy is not strained; / It droppeth as the gentle rain from heaven / Upon the place beneath. It is twice blest; / It blesseth him that gives and him that takes." The sign of true grace in a king, she declares, is not a sceptre in the hand or a crown on the head, but mercy in the heart; for mercy is an attribute of God Himself, and earthly kings are most noble when they temper justice with mercy. "Therefore, Jew," Portia concludes, "consider this, / That in the course of justice, none of us should see salvation. We do pray for mercy / And that same prayer doth teach us all to render / The deeds of mercy." She hopes that he will be moved by these words to renounce his legal claim, but she concludes by saying that if he remains adamant, the Ventian court must pass sentence against Antonio.

COMMENT: This speech of Portia's is undoubtedly the most famous in the play and justly so, for in lyrical verse that is beautiful in itself it clearly states the moral and implies the doctrinal themes of the play: that courtesy teaches the heart to be gentle, that the gentle heart secures salvation, that the stern justice of the Old Law must give way to the mercy of the new, that the Jew must convert to Christianity, by persuasion if possible, by force if necessary.

Portia tells Shylock that what is most admirable in a king is not his power but the humanity with which he exercises this power, repeating the Christian precept also expressed in Shakespeare's Sonnet 94, which begins: "They that have power to do hurt and will do none . . . They rightly do inherit heaven's graces." Until Antonio's bond fell overdue, Shylock was not a man with power to do hurt. Now that he has a chance, however, Portia tries to persuade him to act in such a way as to merit "heaven's graces." She is, in effect, trying to persuade him to convert.

Shylock has emphasized the justice and the legality to his claim to Antonio's flesh. Now, Portia insists that mercy is a higher good than justice, for it ennobles the giver and the receiver. She asks Shylock to consider the thought that if God exacted justice from mankind, no one would get to heaven but in the same remark, she implies that if justice (symbolizing the Old Law) were followed by everyone (as it is by the Jews), then no one would be saved (that is, no one would be a Christian, the only kind of man who can be saved).

Portia has set before Shylock in clear and persuasive terms the moral imperative of Christianity by which he ought to act. Especially as one who has often been at the mercy of other people in the past, Shylock ought now to appreciate the grace-giving quality of mercy. This speech is highly significant in understanding Shakespeare's characterization of the stereotyped Jew. Shylock's heart cannot be moved by this truly effective pleader for the gospel of love and compassion. Now when Shylock proceeds in his cruel demand, Shakespeare shows, it is not for want of having heard such a pleader, but from his own warped nature. Shylock acts deliberately and in full knowledge of what he is doing.

Unmoved by Portia's appeal, Shylock still declares, "I crave the law." The lawyer then asks if Antonio is able to repay the bond, and Bassanio replies that he is ready to pay thrice or even ten times the original sum borrowed. Bassanio argues that if Shylock refuses this offer his only motive can be pure malice, and he begs the court to disregard the law just this once in order to save Antonio. Portia, however, denies this request. She refuses to set the dangerous precedent of ever tampering with the law.

> **COMMENT:** Shakespeare, and his heroine Portia, realize that a strict regard to law is the necessary prerequisite for human society. To break the law once in a good cause is to set a bad example for the future, when the cause may not be so good. Then ends do not justify the means. When Portia finally saves Antonio she will do so within the framework of Venetian law.

Shylock gleefully cries out that the young lawyer is another Daniel come to judge: "O wise young judge, how I do honor thee!" He tells the court that he has sworn an oath to heaven that he will have his bond, and asks whether they think he would risk perjuring himself before God by changing his mind now.

> **COMMENT:** The *Old Testament* name, Daniel, meaning "God is my judge," is associated here with righteous judgment. Daniel was the first judge to introduce cross-examination into trials when he saved Susanna from the false accusations of the Elders. Shylock alludes to the *Old Testament* as may be expected of him. Ironically, this "Daniel" will soon turn his righteous judgment against Shylock.

Portia scrutinizes the bond closely and, finding it all in order, declares that the Jew may have his pound of flesh to be cut off nearest the merchant's heart. Turning to Shylock once more, she asks him to accept the sum of three times his original loan and to bid her tear the bond. He refuses. Antonio, anxious to get his ordeal over with, urges the lawyer to proceed to judgment, and Portia tells the victim to prepare his bosom for the knife. "O noble judge! O excellent young man!" cries Shylock, reminding the court that the bond expressly stipulates that he may take the flesh "Nearest his heart." Portia bids him provide a doctor "for charity" to look after Antonio, but the usurer refuses, objecting that " 'Tis not in the bond."

> **COMMENT:** Our conception of Shylock's cruelty is sharpened when we learn that he had stipulated in the bond that he would claim the pound of flesh from the place nearest Antonio's heart. This gruesome provision reveals a new depth in Shylock's villainy and permits Antonio's grim jest on his debt of friendship in his next speech.

Bidding farewell to Bassanio, Antonio begs his friend not to grieve. He declares that he is well prepared to endure his ordeal, taking comfort in the thought that he will be spared the misery of those men who outlive their wealth and are forced to end their days in cruel poverty. He bids Bassanio convey his greetings to Portia. "Tell her the process of Antonio's end, / Say how I loved you, speak me fair in death / And when the tale is told, bid her be judge / Whether Bassanio had not once a love." In conclusion Antonio swears that as long as Bassanio is truly sorry to see him die, then he for his part does not repent paying his friend's debt "with all my heart."

Bassanio, overwhelmed with grief and frustration, declares that though he dearly loves his wife, he would willingly sacrifice her, or die himself in order to save Antonio. Without revealing her identity, Portia remarks that Bassanio's wife would not be very happy to hear him thus offer her life in sacrifice. Gratiano then declares that he also would gladly see his beloved wife in heaven if she might intercede there for Antonio, and Nerissa remarks that his wife would not take kindly to such an offer. Shylock, who has heard the protestations of these Christian husbands and has taken them literally, declares that he would rather his daughter had married a thief ("any of the stock of Barabbas") rather than a gentile, if this is the kind of love that Christian husbands bear their wives.

> **COMMENT:** Although Antonio has said little in this scene, Portia has spoken for him in her plea for gentle mercy. Now Antonio, in contrast to Shylock's extreme villainy in refusing to provide a surgeon, demonstrates the extreme of charity and friendship in his willingness to die for Bassanio.
>
> There is dramatic irony, a subtle form of humor, in Antonio's desire that Portia "judges" his love for Bassanio, for Portia is presently playing judge and observes Antonio's display of love first hand. The idea of paying the friend's debt "with all my heart," a common metaphor both then and now, is a piece of verbal irony, for in the context of this scene, the statement has literal truth.
>
> The grim humor of Antonio's jest becomes levity in the amusing interpolations by Portia and Nerissa in disguise. They do not interpret their husband's generous offers to sacrifice their wives as literally as does Shylock, who, overhearing the conversation, expresses the belief that Christian husbands actually do sacrifice their wives. If put to the test, however, Christians like Antonio will do a great deal for a friend.

Proceeding to render judgment, Portia declares that the court awards Shylock a pound of flesh to be cut off from Antonio's breast. The Jew, greatly elated, praises this "Most rightful judge," Most learned judge." But his joy is short-lived. Portia then goes on to show that although the bond clearly gives him a pound of flesh, it makes no provision for blood. Therefore, if while claiming his pound of flesh Shylock sheds any Christian blood, he will lose all his possessions to the state in accordance with Venetian law. Now it is Gratiano's turn to gloat and to praise Portia "O upright judge! Mark Jew. O learned judge."

> **COMMENT:** Shakespeare has skillfully built up the tension until it reaches its peak at this point in the play when Portia finally declares that the Venetian law must award Shylock the right to claim

his pound of flesh. But just at the moment when all hope seems lost, the situation is saved by the loophole Portia has discovered in the contract.

Portia allows the court to believe that there is no hope for Antonio in order to test Shylock's resolution. It is her way of giving him every possible chance to change his mind, and, symbolically, to convert. She tries to appeal to Shylock's mercy, to his avarice, then to both. Next, she asks for a surgeon out of charity and is denied. Failing of these appeals, she invokes the letter of the law against Shylock. In other words, she first uses every means of persuasion open to her in Christian doctrine and human nature then she deals with Shylock on his own ground. Using literal interpretation of his bond, she thwarts his vengenance and turns the tables against him.

Surprised by this turn of events, Shylock declares his willingness to accept Bassanio's offer of three times the original value of the bond, but now Portia will not let the matter rest. She declares that since he asked for justice he shall get nothing but justice, that is, his pound of flesh, and warns him that if he takes either slightly more or less than just a pound he will lose all his property and will be condemned to death. Again Gratiano crows with delight, imitating Shylock's earlier praise of the lawyer: "A second Daniel! A Daniel, Jew!"

Hoping to salvage at least his original investment, Shylock declares himself willing to accept the original three thousand ducats, but again Portia insists that he shall get nothing but the forfeit. Shylock then decides to abandon his claim, and prepares to leave the court, when Portia tells him of the Venetian law that says if an alien is found guilty of attempting the life of any citizen, his property shall be divided evenly between the intended victim and the state. Furthermore, his life shall be at the mercy of the Duke to dispose of. Shylock is clearly guilty under this law and Portia advises him to bow before the Duke and humbly to seek mercy. Gratiano, delighted by this news, enjoys taunting Shylock in his humiliation.

COMMENT: Shylock had only considered the letter of the law in calling for justice, while Portia had implored him to obey its spirit. She knew, however, that if Shylock went ahead with his intention, he would be guilty of violating Venetian statutes. She herself was showing mercy by offering Shylock a way out before he proved unremittingly his guilt of attempting a citizen's murder. Grationo's gleeful exclamations reflect the feelings of the Elizabethan audience, that delighted in seeing the villain foiled.

Before Shylock has a chance to say a word, the Duke pardons his life to show him "the difference of our spirit." He decrees that half the usurer's wealth must go to Antonio, but offers to reduce the debt to the state to a small fine. Shylock, however, is hardly grateful for this concession. "Nay, take my life," he tells the Duke, for without his wealth he cannot earn a living, and he feels he might just as well die now as starve in the course of time.

Portia then asks Antonio what mercy he can render Shylock. Gratiano mutters his hope that Antonio will offer nothing more than a free halter for the Jew to hang himself, but Antonio is a more generous spirit. He asks the Duke to let Shylock keep one half his possessions, allowing Antonio the use of the other half until death, when it will go to Lorenzo and Jessica. The merchant also stipulates that Shylock must convert to Christianity and must make Lorenzo his legal heir. The Duke heartily approves these proposals and declares he will revoke his pardon if Shylock does not agree, whereupon Shylock consents. Portia bids the clerk draw up the deed of gift to his heirs for him to sign. Shylock, feeling ill by now, asks leave to go home and to have the deed sent after for him to sign. The Duke grants this request, and as Shylock leaves, Gratiano declares that if he had been judge he would have sent the Jew to the gallows rather than to the baptismal font.

COMMENT: The Duke and Antonio show Shylock "the difference of our spirit" by treating him with the Christian mercy that he refused to grant Antonio. They not only spare his life, but also spare him the poverty to which a strict adherence to the law would have reduced his estate. No "eye for an eye and a tooth for a tooth" justice for these truly Christian gentlemen. As in Portia's speech, "The quality of mercy is not strained" with them "it droppeth as the gentle rain from heaven," even before it is solicited.

Earlier, Shylock declared that he is no different from the Christians in seeking vengeance upon his enemies. "If a Jew wrong a Christian, what is his humility, Revenge. If a Christian wrong a Jew, what should his sufferance be by Christian example? Why, Revenge. The villainy you teach me I will execute, and it shall go hard but I will better the instruction." At the conclusion of this trial scene, however, we see that Shylock's picture of Christian vengeance does not apply to Antonio and the Duke, who are ideal gentlemen.

Gratiano, on the other hand, expresses the public's attitude toward Jews, which was far from ideal. Throughout the trial, he has acted toward Shylock as Shylock has acted toward Antonio, with hatred, contempt, and a total lack of charity. Like Shylock, Gratiano wants the full weight of the law to crush his enemy. He urges the Duke and Antonio to show the Jew no mercy, and as Shylock leaves the courtroom utterly defeated and feeling ill, Gratiano taunts him by wishing him the gallows rather than the baptismal font. The low-comic impulse of the Shakespearean audience is thus satisfied by having the Jew as a butt and a convert at the same time.

The conditions that Antonio imposes on Shylock are kind and generous ones from the Christian point of view. Antonio would have

Shylock behave naturally toward his daughter by having him leave her husband his wealth. We have already seen how deserving of good fortune the gentle Christian couple are.

The Duke and Antonio, in forcing Shylock to choose death or conversion, believe it is a kindness to provide for the Jew's salvation. As a convert, Shylock gets life and eternal life in exchange for the death and eternal damnation, which are his if he remains a Jew.

The Duke invites Portia to dinner, but the "lawyer" politely declines, explaining that "he" must return to Padua immediately. The Duke exists, and Bassanio offers the lawyer a fee of three thousand ducats, which Portia refuses, declaring: "He is well paid that is well satisfied / And I, delivering you, am satisfied." She wants no monetary reward and simply says "I pray you know me when we meet again," (the true meaning of which only she and Nerissa understand). Bassanio, however, insists upon her taking some remembrance, as a gift if not as a fee, and Portia agrees to accept his gloves. When her husband takes off his gloves, she notices his ring and says she will take that. Bassanio, greatly distressed, tries to dissuade her, arguing that the ring is worthless, and offers to find out the most precious ring in Venice instead. When Portia insists on having this one, he finally explains that it was given him by his wife, who made him vow neither to sell, nor to give, nor lose it. The lawyer then accuses Bassanio of selfishness and hypocrisy for refusing to part with the one insignificant trifle she requests. Knowingly, Portia declares that if Bassanio's wife were not insane and if she knew what the lawyer had done for Antonio, she would not begrudge her husband's parting with the ring. With these words Portia and Nerissa exit.

COMMENT: Portia naturally has no interest in monetary payment for her services, but she is playfully curious to test her husband's estimate of his wife. Will he obey her command literally? Does he think she is a madwoman who will not forgive him? She does her best to make him feel badly for refusing to surrender the ring. When Bassanio remains steadfast in spite of her arguments, Portia departs. She may be pleased with his loyalty but she is not pleased with his literal obedience to her command, for we must know by now that Portia values the spirit of the word far above literal fidelity to a promise.

Antonio, chagrined at Bassanio's refusal to give the ring to the lawyer, tells his friend to change his mind: "Let his deservings and my love withal, / Be valued 'gainst your wife's commandments." Bassanio, persuaded, sends Gratiano with the ring after the two young women to request them to come to Antonio's house, where the gentlemen intend to spend the night before setting out early in the morning for Belmont.

COMMENT: Although Bassanio has been proof against the doctor's urgings, he cannot hold out when Antonio tells him to break his wife's "commandments," a word which should remind us of the trial scene just past, with its issue over literal and spiritual interpretation of law. The ring seems a small sacrifice to make compared with all that his friend has been willing to do for him, and the breaking of a "commandment" in the spirit of love will surely be forgiven mercifully.

SUMMARY. This scene, by far the longest in the play, is also the climax of the drama. The conflict between Antonio and Shylock, which represents the conflict between two religions and two ways of life, finally comes to a head and is resolved. The action of this courtroom scene can be divided into four parts: first, Shylock's inexorability before the Duke and Bassanio; second, Portia's ineffectual appeal to the Jew to show mercy to his intended victim; third, the resolution of the dispute in Antonio's favor by means of Portia's legal acumen, and the triumph of the *New Testament* and Good (the spirit of law) over the *Old Testament* and evil (the letter of the law); and finally, the problem of whether Bassanio should reward the lawyer with his precious ring. The crisis builds up in the first two parts of the scene as our concern for Antonio's safety increases. In the third part the tension is relieved, and in the fourth part the play returns to romantic comedy where it started and where it will end in the following act.

In this scene the two central characters of the play, the merciful Portia and the heartless Shylock, confront each other for the first and only time, and our attention is focused chiefly on them.

All appeals to Shylock's Christian charity fail, for he has none. Finally, Portia must resort to literalness herself. She turns Antonio over to Shylock's knife and then, surprisingly, turns on the usurer and has him charged with attempting the life of a Venetian citizen. Portia, disguised as a doctor of law, bears the entire responsibility for saving Antonio's life. She does her utmost to persuade Shylock to relent (symbolically, to convert), but when he fails to do so, she shows what a boomerang the law can be to those who insist on the letter and not the spirit of the law. Ultimately, Shylock is treated with Christian mercy, which includes a fine, the forefit of half his money, and his conversion to Christianity. The forced conversion is a logical consequence of Portia's eloquent and rational pleading, which proved to the Christian mind that persuasion was ineffectual and that force was the only means of dealing with a stubborn Jew.

The difference among the three Venetian friends, Antonio, Bassanio, and Gratiano, is nowhere clearer than in this scene. Antonio is calmly resigned to his fate, and his gentle melancholy and devoted friendship reflect the nobility of his soul. Bassanio is extremely concerned for Antonio, but although he loses his temper, he never loses his dignity as Gratiano does. Gratiano still behaves like a fool. Although motivated by noble feelings of friendship, his hissing of the villain fails to dignify his noble feelings, and his uncharitable outbursts and malicious sentiments toward Shylock show his kinship with the rabble.

The atmosphere of hatred is dispelled when Shylock leaves the stage and we return to the romantic affairs of Portia, who is trying to trick her husband out of a ring. Antonio's friendship prevails with Bassanio over his wife's command.

Act Four, Scene Two

The scene is another street in Venice, and Portia is bidding her "clerk" bring the deed of gift to Shylock for his signature. Gratiano comes upon them, bringing with him Bassanio's ring for "the lawyer" as well as an invitation to dinner. Portia declines the dinner but accepts the ring with thanks. She asks Gratiano to show her "youth" the way to Shylock's house, and when he agrees Nerissa whispers to Portia that she will try to get from her husband the ring she made him swear to keep forever. Portia replies, also in a whisper, that Gratiano will surely part with his ring too. She predicts that in Belmont their husbands will swear that they gave the rings to men, "but we'll outface them, and outswear them too." Nerissa and Gratiano exit one way, while Portia goes another, having planned to meet her maid shortly.

COMMENT AND SUMMARY: This very brief scene is important primarily in preparing us for the romantic comedy of the next and final act. For one thing, we see that Portia will bring back to Belmont with her the deed of gift for Lorenzo, which will gladden his heart. More significant, however, we see that Portia is sure that since Bassanio parted with his ring, Gratiano will follow suit. She is aware that servants and friends imitate the manners of their betters, and she approves of the gentle jest which Nerissa undertakes. Nerissa's desire for the ring, of course, is merely a desire to emulate her mistress.

Act Five, Scene One

Back in Belmont, Lorenzo and Jessica are enjoying a beautiful moonlit night. "The moon shines bright. In such a night as this, / When the sweet wind did gently kiss the trees / And they did make no noise, in such a night / Troilus methinks mounted the Troyan walls, / And sighed his soul toward the Grecian tents / Where Cressid lay that night," Lorenzo muses aloud, and Jessica, following his train of thought, fancies that on such a night Thisbe must have gone to her tryst with her lover Pyramus, when, frightened by a lion, she ran home again. Lorenzo thinks of Dido mourning after Aeneas, and Jessica imagines Medea gathering enchanted herbs to save her lover Jason. Finally Lorenzo says that on such a night, "Did Jessica steal from the wealthy Jew, / And with an unthrift love did run from Venice / As far as Belmont"; to which his wife teasingly replies that on such a night did young Lorenzo swear he loved her well, deceiving her with false vows of faith. Lorenzo replies that on such a night did Jessica slander her love but he forgave her.

COMMENT: The strident voice of Shylock has been silenced. Portia is on her way home, bringing promise of comedy over the ring. A lull settles over Belmont as two young lovers look at the moon. Beauty and happiness thrive in the enchanted world of Belmont where the play will end, as fairy tales do, with the promise that all will live happily ever after.

Up to this point, Lorenzo and Jessica have been kept in the background, but now they establish the mood of idyllic pearce and harmony in which the comedy will come to an end. The poetry is Shakespeare at his lyrical best. Through Lorenzo's words, we feel the balmy air, hear the faint wind stirring through the trees, and see the moonlight silvering over the entire scene. The young lovers, delighting in each other and in the beauty of the night, recall the ill-fated lovers of famous mixed couples of classical tradition, all of whom failed of achieving the ideal and constant love which Lorenzo and Jessica have. Troilus, prince of Troy, is seen mourning for Cressida, who has defected to the Greek camp and never will return. Thisbe, in love with Pyramus, the son of a hostile family, is depicted at the fearful moment when she flees the lion and drops her veil. (Supposing her dead when he finds the veil stained by blood of the lion's prey, Pyramus kills himself; later Thisbe comes upon his body and falls upon her lover's sword.) Dido, Queen of Carthage, is seen waving a willow (symbol of forsaken love) after Aneas has gone to meet his destiny in Rome. And Medea, the barbarian bride of the Greek prince Jason, is seen in a vignette, in which, out of love for her husband, she restores his father's youth, only to be cast aside later.

The misfortunes of these pagan lovers are recalled by way of contrast to Jessica and Lorenzo, who are emblems of "unthrift" (gentle, generous) love in the Christian tradition. This entire scene is notable for its numerous allusions to pagan mythology, which Renaissance philosophers interpreted allegorically in terms of neo-Platonic Christian values. These classical allusions enhance the atmosphere already created by the moonlight, music, and lyrical verse, and reinforce the theme of perfect Christian love which prevails in this last act.

The still of the night is interrupted by the arrival of Portia's servant Stephano, who brings words that his mistress and Nerissa are returning from the monastery and will be home before daybreak. Stephano is immediately followed by Launcelot who arrives crying, "Sola, sola! wo ha! ho sola, sola!" (imitating the sound of a post horn) and announces that a post (messenger) has just brought a "horn full of good news" (with a play on "cornucopia") that Bassanio will be home by morning. Lorenzo bids Stephano report these tidings indoors and send out the house musicians to play in the air.

Alone with Jessica again, Lorenzo re-establishes lyrical mood disrupted by the hurried arrival of the messengers, "How sweet the moonlight sleeps upon this bank! / Here will we sit and let the sounds of music /

Creep in our ears; soft stillness and the night / Become the touches of sweet harmony." He bids Jessica sit and look at the sky, which he calls the "floor of heaven" inlaid with "patterns of bright gold." He reminds her that "there's not the smallest orb which thou behold'st / But in his motion like an angel sings; / Still quiring to the young-eyed cherubins; / Such harmony is in immortal souls, / But whilst this muddy vesture of decay / Doth grossly close it in, we canot hear it."

The musicians enter and as they play Jessica remarks, "I am never merry when I hear sweet music." This her husband explains is because her soul is attentive. He reminds her that music affects even the wildest of animals, which is why legend tells that Orpheus (son of Apollo and consummate musician) could bend to his spell trees, stones and floods. Nothing in nature is insensible to "the sweet power of music." "The man that hath no music in himself, / Nor is not moved with concord of sweet sounds, / Is fit for treasons, stratagems, and spoils; / The motions of his spirit are dull as night, / And his affections dark as Erebus. / Let no such man be trusted. Mark the music."

COMMENT: Lorenzo's sensibility to beauty reveals the soul of a poet in what had seemed to be a quiet and plain young man. His reference to the music made by the heavenly bodies must be understood in the context of the Ptolemaic theory of astronomy that prevailed in Shakespeare's time. It was believed then that the stars moved around the earth, which was thought to be the center of the world, and as they moved they produced celestial music, audible only to the angels and to the souls of men in heaven. This divine music sounded the harmony of the universe and had its counterpart on earth in the voices and instruments sounded by men.

The musical harmony of the spheres, as a manifestation of universal order and unity, cosmic and earthly, in which God created heaven and earth, was a basic assumption among Elizabethans and was rarely explained, except in instructional literature, because it was such a familiar concept. Lorenzo, speaking to his Jewish wife, gives expression to the concept of the correspondence and unity of all things in nature and in heaven. He speaks as a poet in love and also as the instructor of Jessica in the gentle ways of life.

He explains to Jessica that the sadness she feels when listening to music is the hearkening of her soul to the celestial powers which quiet the passions and bring the soul peace and rest. This is what pagan writers meant when they showed that all things in nature, birds, beasts, even trees, became still at the sound of music. In this way, Lorenzo explains the Christian allegory of pagan myth to his untutored wife. He goes on to teach her that the man who does not love music signifies that his soul is not attuned to heavenly beauty, that it cannot rest, that it is on the road to hell (Erebus), and that it is, perhaps, incapable of salvation.

(Shylock, we may recall, hated the "vile squealing of the wry-necked fife," and the "sound of shallow foppery" [II.ii]. The savage beasts that prove tractable under the influence of Orpheus' harmony are more natural in this respect than Shylock.)

While the music is playing, Portia and Nerissa enter. Perceiving the light thrown by the small candle burning in her hall, Portia remarks, "So shines a good deed in a naughty world." When Nerissa observes that the candle was not visible as long as the moon was shining, her mistress answers, "So doth the greater glory dim the less. / A substitute shines brightly as a king / Until a king be by," and then his state seems paltry indeed as does a brook to the "main of waters." The music coming from her house now at night, sounds sweeter to her than it does by day, and she observes that nothing is absolutely good merely in itself, without reference to the circumstances. If the nightingale should sing by day, she would be considered no better a musician than a wren. "How many things by season seasoned are / To their right praise and true perfection!/ Peace! (music ceases) How the moon sleeps with Endymion, / And would not be awakened."

COMMENT: Portia is no less sensitive than Lorenzo to the religious sentiment that "soft stillness and the night / Become the touches of sweet harmony."

She too believes there is a chain of correspondences among all things and that each thing has its proper place and its own perfection. The candle glowing in her hall reminds Portia that a good deed (the saving of Antonio) goes a long way but not very far when considered in relation to celestial bodies, to the state, and to nature itself. The moon, at its end of the ladder of perfection, obscures the glow of its humble counterpart, the candle; the king outshines his substitute; the sea swallows up the brook. In Portia's mind, every creature in the entire design of nature reflects the perfect order of the universe, having its own place and function for making its contribution to the beauty of the world.

Portia's allusion to Endymion, the youth who sought perfect beauty and became the beloved of the moon goddess Selene, is in keeping with the romantic and religious mood established by Lorenzo and Jessica.

Recognizing Portia's voice, Lorenzo welcomes her home and she explains that she and Nerissa have been praying for their husbands' welfare which, they hope will be "the better for our words." (In fact, their husbands are very much the better for Portia's words spoken in the court of Venice, but Lorenzo thinks she is referring to the efficacy of prayer.) She has just time enough to ask that no one tell Bassanio that she has been away, when trumpets announce his arrival. By now the sky is growing light, and Bassanio greets his wife, saying that as long as she is present it is daylight for him even in the darkest night. To this Portia gayly replies, "Let me give light, but let me not be light / For a light wife doth make a heavy husband / And never be Bassanio so for me." (She is punning on the word "light," which meant "bright" and "unfaithful." She cordially welcomes the new arrivals, especially Antonio, declaring her intention of making him feel welcome more by deeds than by words.

COMMENT: Portia and Nerissa deliberately made all haste to return to Belmont before their husbands, for they do not want their joke to be marred by an suspicion of the truth on the part of the men. As we see, they have managed to arrive with not a moment to spare. Portia's entry dispels the lyrical atmosphere of the scene and introduces through her wit, the sophisticated and spirited comedy of the ring which follows.

Nerissa and Gratiano have been talking apart when suddenly a quarrel develops, for Nerissa has noticed that her husband's ring is missing. He swears that he gave it to the judge's clerk, and wishes the young man were "gelt" (castrated) rather than that his wife should be so disturbed. Justifying himself to Portia, Gratiano explains that it was just a "paltry ring" engraved with commonplace poetry, "Love me and leave me not." Nerissa, angry that he should speak so slightingly of the value of the ring and of the quality of the poetry, reminds him of his oath to wear it to his grave. She pretends to believe that he gave it to some other woman, but Gratiano swears he gave it to a youth, "A kind of boy, a little scrubbed boy / No higher than thyself."

Portia reproves Gratiano for parting with his wife's first gift and tells him she is positive that not for all the wealth in the world would Bassanio give away the ring she gave him.

At this, Basanio remarks in an aside that had better cut off his left hand to conceal the truth from her, but too late, Gratiano tells all. Bassanio ruefully admits that he too gave away his ring when not other payment would be accepted by the judge. Pretending she is outraged, Portia swears, "By heaven, I will ne'er come in your bed / Until I see the ring," and Nerissa echoes this vow. Poor Bassanio entreats his wife to be reasonable: "If you did know to whom I gave the ring, / If you did know for whom I gave the ring, / And would conceive for what I gave the ring, / And how unwillingly I left the ring / When naught would be accepted but the ring, / You would abate the strength of your displeasure." But Portia will not be so easily reconciled. "If you had known the virtue of the ring / Or half her worthiness that gave the ring, / Or your own honor to contain the ring, / You would not then have parted with the ring." She refuses to believe that any reasonable man would have insisted on being paid with a ring whose chief value was sentimental, and she declares, like Nerissa, that some woman must have gotten the ring. When Bassanio explains that his sense of honor required him to part with the ring for the judge who had saved Antonio's life, Portia warns her husband that she will be just as generous with her favors to the judge as he was. "I'll not deny him anything I have, / No not my body nor my husband's bed"; and Narissa declares she will do likewise. Gratiano, indignant, warns that if his wife plays loose her lover had better watch out, for "I'll mar the young clerk's pen."

COMMENT: There are strong echoes here of the pseudo-legalistic debates held in the twelfth-century courts of love under the auspices of Eleanor of Aquitaine. For their amusement, the ladies of these ancient French courts would hear complaints made by lovers concerning discourtesies, broken vows, or infidelities. The issues would be disputed at some length and the judges would decide the fault as Portia playfully does here.

The imitative behavior of Gratiano and Nerissa augments the comedy of the rings, in which the witty ladies utterly confound their husbands. The ladies make the most of sexual ironies which the Elizabethan audience understood very well. The body and the bed Portia shared with the learned doctor are her own, of course. The ring, which meant "female genitalia" as well as "a circlet worn for ornament," is especially signficant in this reunion of lovers whose marriages have not yet been consummated.

Antonio is miserable at being the cause of this quarrel, but Portia reassures him that he is not at all to blame and is most welcome. Ever the loyal friend, Antonio now offers Portia his soul as bond for Bassanio's future fidelity, just as formerly he offered his body as bond to Shylock. This suggestion satisfies Portia, who gives Bassanio the ring he gave away to the judge, asking him to keep it more faithfully than before. Her husband recognizes the ring, and in a last bit of teasing Portia tells him that she got it from the judge who lay with her last night, and Nerissa says the same of the clerk. The men are dumbfounded, but before they have time to become very angry, Portia reveals the truth: that she was the doctor and Nerissa the clerk. Relieved and amazed, Bassanio declares, "Sweet doctor, you shall be my bedfellow. / When I am absent, then lie with my wife."

There are other wonders in store. Portia gives Antonio a letter explaining that three of his ships have unexpectedly come to port and that he is once again a wealthy man. Next she gives Lorenzo and Jessica the deed of gift from Shylock, promising that they will be his heirs. Lorenzo with wonder and admiration declares, "Fair ladies, you drop manna in the way / Of starved people."

COMMENT: Report (the gossipy crone of the Elizabethan tavern) has been a liar after all. See III.i.

It is almost morning. Portia suggests that they all go inside where she will answer their questions. As they all exit Gratiano says that his first question will be whether Nerissa would rather remain with the company or go to bed now that it is two hours to day. "But were the day come, I should wish it dark / Till I were couching with the doctor's clerk. / Well, while I live I'll fear no other thing / So sore as keeping safe Nerissa's ring."

COMMENT: After the trial scene in the Fourth Act we may well have wondered how Shakespeare will manage to write an interesting final act that will not be anti-climatic or just dull. The answer is the sophisticated sexual comedy of the rings, which solves the dramatic problem of ending the play. It introduces a note of pretended or apparent discord among the married couples, which increases the surprised delight that accompanies the revelation of the truth and the restoration of perfect harmony in Belmont.

We have already remarked that Portia is a many-sided personality. In the trial scene we saw her maturer qualities: intelligence, eloquence, wit, poise, and deep ethical understanding. Here we see the sophisticated and witty side of the Portia who told her husband (III.ii) that she was "an unlessoned girl, unschooled, unpractised,' and who (III.iv) relished the prospect of dressing up as a youth. Portia has a sense of fun; she can be a bit of a tease, yet she does not lose her sense of proportion; and when she realizes that the joke has gone far enough (that is, when Antonio begins to feel uncomfortable), then she knows it is time to stop. She has never really been angry at Bassanio for giving away the ring; he, for his part, only now learns the truly remarkable character of his new wife, who brings good fortune and good news to every person on stage.

The traditional ending for a comedy is marriage, but in this comedy the wedding took place in the Third Act. What has not yet taken place, however, is the consummation of the marriage, since the husbands had to leave for Venice immediately after the wedding service. The latter part of this scene is full of sexual innuendos and double-entendres (for example, Gratiano's "I'll mar the young clerk's pen"), as well as explicit sexual references (for example, Portia's accusation that Bassanio was unfaithful and her ironic warning that she would deceive him in return). This raciness is definitely in the comic mood that dominates this last act of the play, which now ends with the promise of fidelity in marriage as Portia promises to "answer all things faithfully" and Gratiano suggestively to keep "safe Nerrisa's ring."

SUMMARY. This final scene is important for the following reasons:

1. The essentially comic spirit of the play is restored back in Belmont after the darkly somber implications of the trial scene. We end on a joyous note of universal happiness and well-being, now that Antonio's ships have come safely home, and Lorenzo and Jessica will be heirs to Shylock, and the young husbands and wives are together once more.

2. The first part of the scene contains some beautiful lines of poetry spoken by Lorenzo, whose words evoke the moonlit night of Belmont,

and hymn the power of music to bring heavenly peace to the human and the animal breast. Up till now Lorenzo's character has only been suggested, but he now assumes full shape as a highly poetic, gentle, and spiritual young man in whiose imminent good fortune we rejoice.

3. Portia and Nerissa engage in highly witty sexual play as they reproach their husbands for giving away their rings. The ladies pretend they will be as liberal with their favors (their bodies) as their husbands were with their rings, but when the joke has gone far enough, Portia explains that she and Nerissa were the doctor and the clerk, to the amazement and delight of her hearers. The scene then ends on a merrily salacious note, as all the characters trip off to hear the details of Portia's marvelous disguise.

CHARACTER ANALYSES

ANTONIO, the merchant of the title, is a rich and highly respected citizen in Venice, possessed of many friends. Yet, by nature, Antonio is a melancholy man, a silent and reflective gentleman who values friendship more than anything in the world. His is a gentle and inward melancholy which persists equally when fortune smiles or frowns upon him. He believes that life is a stage on which each man plays his part; reality itself begins in heaven. Nevertheless, Antonio never seeks to dampen the spirits of his gay Venetian friends to suit his own mood, for as an older and more experienced man, he realizes that youth must have its fling. His love for Bassanio is one of the noblest friendships in literature. "My person, my purse, my extremest means," he gladly offers to Bassanio with an unstinting generosity that does not flag when he is finally threatened with death. Antonio never blames Bassanio nor repents his own decision to sign the bond for his friend's sake. Once redeemed, Antonio shows perfect Christian charity, returning good for ill, and showing mercy to Shylock after the latter's inhuman attempt on his life. His call for Shylock's conversion is an act of grace, for the greatest charity a Christian gentleman can do is to help save a man's soul.

The Antonio whom we see on the stage is unfailingly kind and gentle towards his friends and ultimately merciful towards his enemy, but he is also the Antonio whom Shylock describes as spitting upon him and kicking him in public. This is acceptable behavior for a Christian toward a Jew, who, in Elizabethan eyes, was no better than a dog. Who would not spit on a man who makes a profit out of other men's needs (for this is the way Antonio sees Shylock)? Still, it is a measure of Shakespeare's sensibility that he never lets us see Antonio act in this way. Antonio exemplifies the noblest virtues of the perfect Christian gentleman in Renaissance society throughout the play.

BASSANIO, friend to Antonio and later husband to Portia, is also a noble, generous, and honorable young man. He captivates the hearts of two of the most high-minded characters in the play, Antonio and Portia. We learn as soon as we meet him that he has not only already spent his fortune, but is also in debt, principally to Antonio. He is seeking a way to mend his ways, pay his debts, and retrieve his fortune by marrying Portia, whom he loves. His profligacy is to be regarded kindly, for it is a sign of high spirits and noble birth. The young Renaissance gentleman was expected to philander in his youth so that he could learn the evil ways of the world and come to reject them. His choice of Portia as his wife is to be admired, for she is also of noble birth, mind, and beauty. Through her, he will be able to mend his ways, live a blessed life and win eternal salvation.

Bassanio moves in a Christian world where, among gentlemen, generosity is the rule, and where wealth is freely given and accepted among friends. There is nothing miserly about Bassanio. When Gratiano asks for a favor,

Bassanio grants it even before knowing what the favor is (II.ii). As soon as he learns of the peril in which his friend Antonio stands, he hurries to his side. Bassanio's grief and remorse are no less than what we expect of the impassioned friend. He has the goodness of soul which enables him to choose correctly among the three caskets, but he lacks the resourcefulness and wit to find a way out of the bond. In imagination and ethical seriousness, Bassanio is less remarkable than his wife, yet he is the man whom she loves and in whom Belmont will find a noble and honorable lord.

GRATIANO, another Venetian friend, is by nature garrulous, gregarious, and often rather crude. As he himself says, "Let me play the fool, / With mirth and laughter let old wrinkles come / And let my liver rather heat with wine / Than my heart cool with mortifying groans" (I.i). This is the Gratiano who speaks "an infinite deal of nothing." There is a cynically reflective side to him as well, when he muses in a moment of tranquility on the fleeting nature of desire; (II.vi) and he shows generosity later when he appreciates the fact that Jessica must feel strange in Belmont and therefore bids Nerissa make the girl feel at home (III.ii).

Gratiano is to Bassanio what Nerissa is to Portia, a sort of weak echo to the principal romantic lover. Thus Gratiano woos the maid when Bassanio woos the mistress, and when Bassanio gives his ring to the judge, Gratiano gives his to the clerk. Bassanio teaches his friend courtesy, but Gratiano is clearly a less generous man than Bassanio, for he is the only Christian in the trial scene who taunts Shylock and who urges that no mercy be shown him, Although his counsel does not prevail, his spiteful words reflect the popular attitude toward Jews. His is the voice of common humanity, seeking revenge. Finally, Gratiano's racy turn of mind keeps up an undercurrent of sexual innuendo which contributes to the comic spirit of the play.

SALANIO AND SALARINO, friends of Antonio and Bassanio, serve to create the atmosphere of Venice and to advance the plot, but we know almost nothing at all about their personal lives or what sort of men they really are. It is the language of these two men that in the first scene tells us of high masts and proud sails on the merchant ships, of rich and exotic cargoes, of danger on the seas, all of which helps to create a sense of the magnificence and the romance of Venice. It is also from the mouths of these two men that we hear of Shylock's reaction to Jessica's elopement, of his intention to claim his pound of flesh if Antonio fails the payment, and of the various Venetian ships reported lost and very likely including Antonio's. The dialogues between Salanio and Salarino thus take the place of narrative and bridge the gaps in time, which the dramatist does not want to depict on stage. Such friends as there would surely have raised the money to repay Antonio's debt on time if they had had it. We can only assume that, like Bassanio and Lorenzo, they were "unthrifty young gentlemen."

LORENZO, another young Venetian, is a quiet young man who is contrasted by the voluble and loquacious Gratiano early in the play. He has the initiative to plan and execute an elopement with Jessica and offers her constant love. As he tells Launcelot, he is a plain man given to plain speech, by which he means he is not a foolish word-twister. Lorenzo really comes into his own as a romantic and gentle Christian in the last act, when, musing on a moonlit night in Belmont, he reveals his profoundly poetic and religious sensibility to beauty of all kinds, especially to music. He teaches Jessica the ways of earthly and heavenly love, and his good fortune at the end of the play accords with the nobility of his nature.

THE DUKE OF VENICE, as the ruler of his city-state, knows that his first duty is the enforcement of law and the maintenance of order. We hear about him first when Salanio and Salarino describe how Shylock brought him down to the docks to search for Jessica. He appears only once, in the trial scene, where the Duke admits that as head of state he must protect the commercial interests of Venice by upholding the contract for the pound of flesh and tries to persuade Shylock to be merciful. He shows mercy himself by pardoning Shylock his life, reducing his fine, and offering him a chance to convert.

THE PRINCE OF MOROCCO is a comically exotic figure in Belmont, with his dark skin and white robes and his flowery language. At once proud and shy, confident and nervous, the Prince speaks boastfully in the sententious, almost pompous tones of a man who does not quite feel himself accepted in Christian surroundings, as in fact he is not, on account of his religion and color. Failing to perceive the difference between outer show and inner reality, he chooses the gold casket, whose inscription promises what many men desire. The Prince is a ridiculous figure who is politely but coolly dismissed by Portia.

THE PRINCE OF ARRAGON, like the Prince of Morrocco, fails to make the essential distinction required by the ordeal of the caskets: that is, to distinguish between external illusion and internal reality. Arragon is keen enough to discount the fair promise of the gold casket, which he realizes appeals to the "fool multitude." He is an aristocrat who disdains associating with the common herd, but his pride is his undoing, and he is taken in by the inscription on the silver casket, which promises that he will get what he deserves. Because Arragon is sure that he deserves Portia he does not deserve her and does not win her.

SHYLOCK, the Jewish moneylender, is one of the most interesting and one of the most controversial of Shakespeare's characters. Discussion of *The Merchant of Venice* generally centers around Shylock, and yet the play was not called *The Jew of Venice* (a title given to it in 1701), Shylock is not onstage most of the time, and does not appear at all in the final act. Why then do we feel that he is the center of the play? The answer is that Shylock is given the most passionate, most memorable speeches and actions in the play, and his character is etched in bold strokes across its entire surface, leaving an indelible mark on the words and actions of all the other players. He is a believable human being as well as an outrageous villain and comic butt, and has become all things to all men.

Some readers view Shylock as a proud and a passionate man who has long stored up in his heart the humiliation suffered at the hands of the hostile Christian world and is now ready for revenge. But the historical fact is that anti-Semitism was a perfectly acceptable feeling in the sixteenth century, and Shakespeare developed Shylock as the stereotyped comic figure of the villainous Jewish moneylender. Shakespeare was capable, however, of seeing the universal principles of human nature embodied in all men, so that he made Shylock believable as the revengeful Jew. Shylock is the villain of the piece; there is no doubt about that. He hates Antonio for hindering his business and for treating him with terrible contempt in public, and we must not doubt that from the very beginning Shylock had hoped to get his revenge on Antonio by arranging the flesh-bond.

Jessica's elopement and theft of his money and jewels increase Shylock's resentment against the Christian world, so that, although he might have had second thoughts about executing his revenge, he is no longer troubled by them after Jessica's elopement. Having found himself victimized by Antonio, Shylock wants as good as he gets. Symbolizing the stern justice of *Old Testament* law, Shylock is a passionate man thirsting for revenge and the ridiculous figure of stereotyped Jewish obstinacy, hatred, and literalness. Usually comic, he is at times grotesque, and at times even touching ("Hath not a Jew eyes . . ."). He is a villain of perserverence and restless energy, who is, nevertheless, foiled by good Christians in the end.

TUBAL, a Jew and a friend of Shylock, appears only once (III.i), to report the result of his search for the absconded Jessica, but we have already heard of him (I.iii) as the man who will supply Shylock with the funds for Antonio. This Tubal is clearly a serviceable friend, undertaking a trip to Genoa on Shylock's behalf and running to secure the arresting officer for the day that Antonio's bond will fall due. Of the nature of the man himself we know nothing and need to know nothing for the purposes of the drama. In his one appearance, he alternately throws Shylock into despair over Jessica's squandering of the stolen wealth, and then again raises Shylock's hopes that Antonio will be bankrupt. In so doing Tubal helps to emphasize the grotesquely comic aspect of the moneylender.

LAUNCELOT GOBBO, servant to Shylock and then servant to Bassanio, is, as Jessica calls him, "a merry devil." In Shylock's service, he is a rustic who misuses words and plays crude jests. He teases his old father and Jessica in the spirit of fun, but he mocks Shylock with more spite. The fact that Launcelot finds life in Shylock's house so distasteful is a telling factor against the Jew, for in stage tradition such servants were expected to admire and emulate their masters. When Launcelot transfers to Bassanio's service, his crude humor turns to wise foolery and his vocabulary, puns, jests, and ironies become sophisticated. When Launcelot describes the struggle between his conscience and the devil, he reflects the problem Jessica must face: whether to remain with Shylock or to seek a better life with a Christian. Although we never hear Jessica debating this question, we are, in effect, persuaded of the virtue of her decision because we understand the rightness of Launcelot's. Both characters are presumably much better treated and better educated in the households of Christians.

OLD GOBBO, Launcelot's father, appears only once, when he comes bringing a present to his son, whom he at first does not recognize because of his almost total blindness. Like his son, Old Gobbo is a comic rustic figure, constantly mispronouncing or misusing words. Launcelot is under the impression that Old Gobbo was a philanderer in his youth.

PORTIA, the lady of Belmont, is one of Shakespeare's great heroines, whose physical beauty, lively intelligence, quick wit, and high moral seriousness have been nurtured in an atmosphere of wealth and freedom. Like a princess in a fairy tale, she is famed throughout the world for her beauty and her virtue, and her suitors are put to a standard test (the caskets) in order to win her hand. But Portia is no ordinary fairy tale princess. Although she dutifully abides by her father's restrictions concerning her marriage, she is made weary by the necessity to obey. Her satirical comments about her suitors reveal a sharp wit and a keen insight into human nature and suggest that she could choose a husband for herself very well.

It is in the trial scene, however, that we see the full extent of her wit, her intellect, and her charity. Her adventurousness, sureness of purpose, and intelligence save her husband's friend. But Portia is not interested only in saving Antonio; she would like, if possible, also to save Shylock from himself, and to this end she appeals eloquently first to his moral sensibility and than to his avarice. The money that she urges Shylock to accept in lieu of Antonio's flesh is her own money, freely given to Bassanio. For Portia, money cannot be weighed in the balance with a human soul, and when she finally must resort to legal argument in order to rescue Antonio, she still stands for mercy. It is to the ethical preaching of Portia that Shylock owes his life in the end.

While Portia can rise to heights of dignity and eloquence, she remains, after all, a playful and tender wife. Although she dominates the trial scene, we need have no fear that she will overpower her husband at home, for underneath her teasing is a womanly gentleness, an "unschooled" innocence, that promises Bassanio all felicity in his marriage.

NERISSA, Portia's maid, is not so much a servant as a companion who possesses much the same kind of wit and gaiety as her mistress, although she does not demonstrate the ethical concern which ennobles Portia. As

Portia's maid, she emulates her mistress' manners, but she cannot be expected to perceive the inner nature of the gentle heart. Nerissa is to Portia what Gratiano is to Bassanio, a similar but less impressive, less noble edition.

JESSICA, Shylock's daughter, has her father's blood but not his manners. She is a gentle girl who finds life in her father's home unbearably tedious and irksome. It is presumed that she has struggled with her conscience before eloping with Lorenzo, taking with her those jewels and ducats about which Shylock complains. Unlike her father, Jessica does not hesitate to spend money in order to enjoy life. She converts to Christianity under the instruction of Lorenzo and has an eye for the beauty and the harmony which comprises the Christian world view. She is more modest than Portia, who is not embarrassed to wear men's clothing, and she has the perception to notice that Portia is an extraordinary woman, whom she will probably try to emulate.

OTHER MINOR CHARACTERS include **LEONARDO,** servant to Bassanio, and **BALTHASAR** and **STEPHANO,** servants to Portia, as well as various attendants in the court.

CRITICAL COMMENTARY

COMMENTARY ON SHYLOCK. Critical commentary of *The Merchant of Venice* has centered around the character of Shylock, who has been interpreted in various ways, ranging from the comic stereotype of the villainous Jewish moneylender to the tragic victim of age-old persecution.

ROMANTIC INTERPRETATION, Romantic critics who could not accept Shakespeare's anti-Semitism tended to argue that Shylock is really a noble figure of a man, or to emphasize the contumely heaped upon him by the Christian world that preached but, on the whole, did not practice charity. They tended to concentrate on Shylock's speech, "Hath not a Jew eyes. . . ." (II.i) which, they said, reveals Shakespeare's true humanistic outlook that know all men to be essentially the same, despite racial or religious differences. Thus they have sought to explain if not actually to justify the extremity of Shylock's desire for revenge.

The earliest apologist for Shylock was the English Romantic essayist and critic William Hazlitt, who in the early nineteenth century wrote a defense of Shylock as the suffering victim of Chirstian malevolence, Hazlitt reminded his readers that the Jews had long been forced to live in constant fear of being punished, reviled, or burnt alive, and that such fears would sour even the sweetest disposition. "The desire of revenge is almost inseparable from the sense of wrong; and we can hardly help sympathising with the proud spirit, hid beneath his Jewish gaberdine, stung to madness by repeated undeserved provocations, and laboring to throw off the load of obloquy and oppression heaped upon him and all his tribe by one desperate act of 'lawful' revenge, till the ferociousness of the means by which he is to execute his purpose, and the pertinacity with which he adheres to it, turn us against him." Hazlitt, thus, thought of Shylock as taking upon himself the task of avenging his oppressed nation, and for this proud defiance of his allotted role in society Shylock is to be admired. Hazlitt gives Shylock credit for more intelligence, more imagination, and more true strength of character than anyone else in the play.

Later in the nineteenth century, the German poet Heinrich Heine, born a Jew but nominally a Christian, insisted that Shakespeare was not trying to show the difference between two religions but to demonstrate the law of human nature that a man will hate his enemy and seek to execute vengeance on him. Heine conceded that Shakespeare may have originally intended to represent Shylock as a sort of fabulous monster, but that his poetic genius asserted itself, "and so it happened, that in Shylock, in spite of all his uncouth grimacings, the Poet vindicates an unfortunate sect, which for mysterious purposes, has been burdened by Providence with the hate of the rabble both high and low, and has reciprocated this hate—not always by love." Heine acknowledges that Shylock does love money, but he insists that, more than money, the Jew loves his daughter and is cruelly hurt by her desertion. We must hate Shylock but at the same time we cannot help but feel that the man is deeply wronged and is admirable for seeking "righteous retribution" on his enemies.

MODERN INTERPRETATIONS, HISTORICAL vs. ROMANTIC. The Danish critic Georg Brandes, in his essay in 1898, sought to interpret Shylock as the Elizabethan audience would have done, as a comic personage. To the Elizabethan public, Shylock was simply a despised creature, a Jew and a usurer, and his miserliness and his "eagerness to dig for another the pit into which he himself falls" seemed "not terrible but ludicrous." Yet at the same time Brandes felt that Shakespeare himself did not completely share the prejudices of his age, for he showed that Shylock's hardness and cruelty were the result of his passionate nature and of the abnormality of his position in society, "so that in spite of everything, he has come to appear in the eyes of later times as a sort of tragic symbol of the degradation and vengefulness of an oppressed race."

The twentieth-century critic and scholar, Professor E. E. Stoll, refused to distinguish between the reactions of the Elizabethan audience and the original conception in the mind of Shakespeare. Stoll felt that Shakespeare deliberately incorporated all the conventional attitudes towards Jews in the character of Shylock, who consequently emerges as complete villain and comic butt. We must conclude that Shakespeare has no kindly thoughts for Shylock from the following facts: no other character in the play has anything good to say about him, although many (including his daughter and servant who know him well) have unfavorable comments. Secondly, the only time when we might be tempted to feel sorry for Shylock, when his daughter runs away, we are not permitted to see his reaction for ourselves, but are told about it by Salanio and Salarino in such a way that Shylock seems much more monstrous than his daughter. Finally, we are allowed to hear Shylock remark in an aside at the very beginning of the play that he hates Antonio and looks forward to getting revenge on him if he can. The soliloquies and asides in Shakespeare are always indicative of the true feelins of a character. According to Stoll, then, the audience was not meant to commiserate or sympathize with Shylock at any point in the play.

Stoll's position is not accepted by all modern critics. Harley Granville-Barker, in his *Prefaces to Shakespeare*, writes sympathetically of Shylock's grudging affection for Launcelot and of his absolute devotion to his daughter in whom, alone of all the world, he can place his trust and his love. Granville-Barker is willing to make the distinction between the way in which the Venetian gentlemen in the play think of Shylock (the stereotype of the Jewish moneylender) and the way in which the audience is supposed to see Shylock, which is as "all Jewry couched and threatening there, an ageless force behind it." For Granville-Barker, Shylock is a "Puritan stranger in a wastrel world," and his true tragedy lies in the fact that he did not push his reliance on law and the prophets to its extreme by claiming the pound of flesh despite the heavy penalty he would have suffered for doing so. If Shylock had been willing to suffer for his passionate principle of revenge, then he might have emerged as a tragic figure instead of as a weak and vacillating individual.

Another modern critic, John Dover Wilson, tried to show that Shylock demonstrates the "pitiless observation and divine compassion and understanding" which is Shakespeare's great genius. On the other hand, the critic John Palmer (*Comic Characters of Shakespeare,* 1946) believes with E. E. Stoll that anti-Semitism was in fashion during the time that Shakespeare wrote *The Merchant of Venice* and that Shylock was a comic butt from beginning to end. Palmer, however, admits that some Elizabethans must have been sympathetic to the Jews and that we are moved to pity Shylock in the end. According to Palmer, "Shakespeare took the comic Jew for a theme and wrote . . . a comedy in which ridicule does not exclude compassion. . . "

Latching on to the possibility that there was some sympathy for Jews in Elizabethan England, C. N. Coe (*Shakespeare's Villains,* 1957) argues that the character of Shylock is the nearest thing to a psychological study of a villain in Shakespeare, that Shakespeare takes trouble to explain the hatred existing between Antonio and Shylock, that he give reasons for Shylock's hatred, and the he does not have Antonio refute Shylock's charges or attempt a reconciliation. Coe agrees with Palmer and Stoll that Shylock is ridiculous in the scene with Tubal, that his cruelty and meanness are thwarted, making him a comic character, but he feels that Shylock is also the object of pity. The pathetic speech, "Hath not a Jew eyes?", overrides the ridicule. "Considered by himself," Coe writes, "Shylock has appealed to many as one of the finest examples of psychologically accurate characterization which Shakespeare ever achieved." The problem, however, in *The Merchant of Venice* is "that of characterizing the villain so thoroughly that we sympathize with him and can feel little, if any, satisfaction in his punishment." In this respect, Coe agrees with the subjective criticism of Ernest Dowden (1924) whose introduction to his edition of the play included the following judgment: "*The Merchant of Venice* is probably the first of Shakespeare's comedies in which the study of character wholly dominates all other interests."

A most sensible approach to the problem of Shylock is expressed by Louis B. Wright in his Folger edition of the play (1960). Wright, an historian and critic of Elizabethan life and literature, writes: "In making Shylock, the moneylender, a member of the Jewish race, Shakespeare was not consciously contributing to anti-Semitism, but he was reflecting a cruelty that persisted from past ages of persecution." Wright goes on to state, "Shakespeare was an artist of extraordinary power, and he was not content to represent Shylock merely as a symbol of evil. As always in his plays, the dramatist gives his characters life, and Shylock, who might have become merely the representation of an abstract vice in the hands of a lesser dramatist, becomes in Shakespeare's recreation a man who has suffered much, whose hatred is explained by the treatment he and his whole race have had to endure. He is the symbol of Hate, it is true, but Hate induced by injustice and humiliation."

The fact that different critics have found such different Shylocks in the one character is a tribute to Shakespeare's ability to create a real human being whose complexity cannot be obscured by calling him either a "tragic figure" or "comic villain." Shylock is neither simply a monster nor the noble victim of persecution. He is a combination of many qualities that are themselves affected by the circumstances in which he finds himself.

CRITICISM ON MINOR CHARACTERS. Since critical controversy has centered around the character of Shylock, commentary on the other characters has tended to fall into line with the basic attitude of the critic towards Shylock. Those critics who think of the Jew as a deeply injured man (such as Hazlitt and Heine) tend to criticize Jessica for her callousness towards her father, to blame Lorenzo for complacently stealing the Jew's daughter and money, and to deprecate Antonio as a weak-spirited creature and Bassanio as a fortune hunter bent on marrying a rich heiress. On the other hand, those critics who see Shylock as a hard-hearted villain tend to vindicate the characters who are in opposition to him.

Portia, the other central character of the play, has been regarded on the whole as one of the most charming and intelligent of Shakespeare's heroines. Hazlitt, who was not so favorably impressed, criticized her for pedantry and affectation, maintaining that "although her speech about mercy is all very well . . . there are a thousand finer ones in Shakespeare." Other critics, however (including Heine), have tended to agree with Mrs. Anna Jameson's evaluation in her book, *Shakespeare's Heroines* (1833). Mrs. Jameson speaks of Portia's combination of womanly grace, intellectual acumen, and spirit of adventure, and emphasizes that nobility of spirit which seeks to find in Shylock some trace of compassion that would make him worthy of her generosity.

PROBLEM OF GENRE. The problem of genre seems to have existed from the very moment that the play was produced. Elizabethans were having trouble themselves distinguishing the genres, a classical idea (which had been revived in England not long before Shakespeare's time) requiring that plays follow certain rules for comedy or tragedy, never mixing the two. There was no genre called "history" among the ancients and certainly nothing resembling "comicall historie," which was the caption and running title of the first quarto edition of *The Merchant* (1600). The editions of 1619, 1623, 1637, and 1652 retained the disignation "comicall historie," but French classical criticism which encumbered English thought in the last half of the seventeenth century made such a designation totally untenable. In fact, the play itself could not be left in its mixed condition and was rewritten by George Granville Lord Lansdowne in 1701 as *The Jew of Venice, alter'd from Shakespeare*. Granville's version was a clear-cut comedy in which Shylock was the object of ridicule. (Jews by that time had returned to England.)

In 1709, Nicholas Rowe, the first of the eighteenth century editors of Shakespeare, challenged the designation of *The Merchant* as a comic play. "Though we have seen the Play Received and Acted as a Comedy," said Rowe, "and the part of the Jew performed by an excellent Comedian, yet I cannot but think it was designed Tragically by the Author. There appears in it such a deadly Spirit of Revenge, such a savage Fierceness and Fellness, and such a bloody designation of Cruelty and Mischief which cannot agree either with the Stile or Characters of Comedy."

Despite Rowe's subjective and romantic protest, *The Merchant* continued to be played and printed as a comedy during the eighteenth century. The 1777 actor's edition of the Theatres-Royal in Drury-Lane and Covent-Garden, for example, ignored early suggestions of a history genre and played it simply as *The Merchant of Venice. A Comedy.*

An undated nineteenth century edition published by the National Acting Drama Office in London courageously challenged its predecessors by entitling the play *The Merchant of Venice; a Tragedy in Five Acts.* Several nineteenth century versions edited by George Daniel appeared under the cautious label, *The Merchant of Venice; a Play in Five Acts.* For the most part, however, the designation "comedy" has stuck, even in the nineteenth century when sentimental and humanitarian feeling for Shylock was at its highest.

In our own century, the genre originally assigned to the play accords with modern historical views of the character of Shylock. Stoll and Palmer, for example who conceive of Shylock primarily as a comic character, very naturally assume the play is a comedy. Even those who see tragic overtones in the characterization of the usurer agree that the play is comedy. W. W. Lawrence (*Shakespeare's Problem Comedies* 1931) excludes *The Merchant* from the class of problem comedies, in which the problem mood must dominate the action, because he views the Shylock-Antonio plot, the clash between Jew and Gentile, as "only a part of the complicated action . . . which taken as a whole must clearly be classified as romantic comedy."

The puzzling genre is perhaps best described by Tucker Brooke (*The Renaissance,* 1948), who calls *The Merchant* "one of the gravest of comedies, and capable of being misread as a tragedy. It is, likewise, a play of motley ingredients and Gothic atmosphere, and has no particular congener in the Shakespeare canon."

ESSAY QUESTIONS AND ANSWERS

1, Does Portia break the rules of the lottery and help Bassanio choose the right casket?

ANSWER: The question has often been raised whether or not Portia has betrayed her father by giving Bassanio strong hints as to the correct casket in the song that is played during his choosing. It has been suggested, for example, that the first three lines of the song end with words rhyming with "lead" ("bred," "head," "nourished") and suggests the correct answer to Bassanio. The rhymes are accidental, or if they do suggest "lead," the suggestion is purposely misleading, for if Bassanio associated the lead box with Fancy, he would certainly never choose it. Every perfect courtier-scholar of the Renaissance world knew that Fancy was a fickle kind of love not rooted in the "constant soul," that it was bred in the head, not in the heart. (Portia had already stated that he who chose by wit would lose by it, II.ix. 80, implying that the heart must be the guide to the prize.) It was understood among the gentle elite of Tudor England that, as the song said, Fancy was a short-lived kind of love, engendered in the eye, based only on the appearance of things, and quickly surfeited before it ever reached the heart. The suggestion that the riddle-song actually makes is that Bassanio choose out of love, not Fancy, or that he be not deceived by appearances as those who choose Fancy are. This hint, however, would be of no use to the man who could not distinguish between Fancy and permanent love.

The song does indeed hint at the correct choice, but the hint is not a betrayal of her father's wishes. It is clear that Portia understands the reason for the lottery. Her father had wished her to have a constant husband, one who was imbued with the proper virtues of the perfect Christian gentleman. No suitor lacking in these virtues could pass the test of the caskets, nor could the vain and the foolish suitor know where Fancy is bred, or correctly interpret hints that Portia may offer. Only the perfectly devoted lover of courtly tradition would refuse to be deceived by the outer appearance of things and would be willing to hazard all for the lady he loves.

Bassanio learns the answer to the riddle without the aid of the song. In fact, he is so preoccupied examining his heart for the correct decision, he may not even hear the song. We may even imagine that the song is used, not as a hint to Bassanio, but as a musical background reflecting the very thoughts in Bassanio's mind.

2. What are Shylock's motives for his hatred of Antonio?

ANSWER: Before Shylock ever says a word to Antonio, he lets the audience know in an aside that he hates Antonio for having hindered his business (by lending money without interest charges) and for having humiliated him in public by spitting upon him and calling him names such as "dog" and "cutthroat Jew." In this aside, Shylock says he hopes to get revenge on Antonio both for his own humiliation and for the persecution that the Jews have long suffered at the hands of Christians. After delivering this aside, Shylock then tells the Christian gentlmen that he wants to be friends with them and will conclude the bond for a pound of flesh as a "merry sport." In the second act, however, he still seems to bear a deep grudge against the Christians, for he tells Jessica that he is going in hate and not in friendship to feed upon them (that is, to dine with Bassanio), and he adds his hope that Launcelot will help to waste Bassanio's money. After Jessica's elopement, Shylock suspects Bassanio and Antonio of abetting her escape, and this suspicion increases Shylock's animosity toward Antonio. We learn later in the play that Antonio has personally rescued a number of debtors from Shylock's clutches and that Shylock cannot nor will not explain his reasons for demanding Antonio's flesh. "But say it is my humor," is all the reason he is able to show. A major cause of Shylock's hatred, however, is amply demonstrated although briefly stated. He hates Antonio, whom he calls a "fawning publican," because he is a Christian (I.iii). The sum of Shylock's motives for hatred is given in the rarely quoted lines preceding the famous "Hath not a Jew eyes": "He hath disgraced me, and hind'red me half a million; laughed at my losses, mocked at my gains, scorned my nation, thwarted my bargains, cooled my friends, heated mine enemies—and what's his reason? I am a Jew."

3. In what ways are we made to feel some degree of sympathetic understanding for Shylock's passion for revenge?

ANSWER: In the first act, when Shylock says that Antonio has spit upon him and called him names in public and hindered his business, we must feel to some extent that the Jew has been wronged, even though we know that he has also wronged others. We know that Jews in that period of history were severely persecuted, confined to life in a ghetto, prohibited from engaging in many occupations and, therefore, often forced to resort to usury as a means of earning a livelihood. We are bound to feel some sympathy for Shylock, whose very clothing and customs, quite apart from his religion, make him an alien figure and a suspicious character on the steets of Venice. When Jessica runs away from home we realize that Shylock's most trusted prop has failed him, for he reposed absolute confidence in his daughter even if he did not make her life a happy one at home. The fact that he cries out for his ducats as well as his daughter should not obscure the sense of keen personal loss. Our sympathy for Shylock is at its height when we hear him deliver the famous speech: Hath not a Jew eyes? Hath not a Jew hands and all the other faculties and sensibilities common to all mankind? At this point, it seems that, essentially, Shylock is no different from any other man except that the accident of his religion has made him an outcast from society. Our understanding of this fact does not mitigate our horror at his cruelty towards Antonio, but we are able to remember that the passion for revenge is a commmon human failing and not the unique characteristic of a ferocious and inhuman monster as the Elizabethans believed.

4. Why does Portia wait such a long time in the trial scene before she reveals the legal loophole that will free Antonio from Shylock's clutches?

ANSWER: For one thing, the tense and long drawn-out trial scene makes for very effective drama. But there is a more important reason why Shakespeare made Portia delay in giving Shylock the *coupe de grace*. In a word, Portia wants to save Shylock from himself by having him relent of his own accord and by proving that he does have compassion for human suffering. Symbolically, she wants him to convert to Christianity and to gentle ways of his own accord. Portia wants to win a moral victory rather than a legal victory. If she can get Shylock to acknowledge that the spirit of the law is mercy and win him away from his literal interpretation of the law, she will have succeeded in making a Jew think like a Christian. To this end, she appeals to Shylock first on the *New Testament* grounds that mercy is a divine attribute, blessing both those who give and those who receive; then by appealing to his human avarice and offering extra money in return for a dismissal of the case against his friend. But as the stereotype of the inhuman Jew, Shylock remains impervious to Portia's appeal to the Christian charity and human greed which Shylock does not have. He prefers the unnatural satisfaction of claiming the pound of flesh to pocketing even six times the original three thousand ducats, which Portia generously urges upon him. Only when Portia has exhausted every means of persuasion does she finally deal with Shylock in his own terms. She resorts to the letter of the law to prevent him from executing vengeance upon Antonio. Her eloquence and her Christian generosity are not equal to moving his hard Jewish heart.

Portia's appeal to Shylock is developed at considerable length in order to show her Christian patience, mercy, and generosity in contrast to Shylock's Jewish literalness, inhumanity, and hatred. As Christian propaganda, this scene proves that Jews will not listen to reason and that forced conversion is necessary if harmony is to be restored to the Christian world.

5. What is the dramatic function served by Salanio and Salarino?

ANSWER: In the very first scene, Salanio and Salarino help to create our sense of the atmosphere of Venice by their elaborate descriptions of the ships that ply the seas loaded with their exotic cargoes. Their imagery conjures up for us a resplendent Venice thriving on a glamorous commerce with the romantic Orient. In the later scenes of the play Salanio and Salarino take the place of a narrator or chorus, for it is in the course of their conversations that certain aspects of the plot are advanced without being dramatized. It is through Salanio and Salarino that we learn of Shylock's reaction to Jessica's elopement: his wild outcries for his daughter and his ducats, and his suspicion that Bassanio and Antonio conspired with Lorenzo in the escape. It is also through Salanio and Salarino that we hear the first rumor of a Venetian ship lost at sea and later hear of others. Finally, Salanio and Salarino are used to provide narrative descriptions of Antonio and Shylock and the judgments with which we are expected to evaluate these characters.

6. In what way are Jessica and Lorenzo, both separately and together, a commentary on Shylock and his way of life?

ANSWER: Although Jessica is Shylock's daughter, she seems to have adopted none of his manners. Whereas Shylock wants to keep a "sober" house, free from mirth and music, Jessica has a good sense of humor, and enjoys the wit of the "merry devil" Launcelot, who provides the only ray of sunshine in her gloomy house; and she enjoys the sweet harmony of music. Whereas Shylock is close-fisted, Jessica freely spends what money she has to make life gay and beautiful. Then again, while Shylock hates and fears the Christian world, Jessica has fallen in love with one Christian in particular and with the gracious and bountiful life that is led by all the Christians in the play. Her father converts to Christianity under duress, but Jessica does so voluntarily in response to her love for Lorenzo.

Lorenzo, for his part, shows that the Christian world is not unalterably hostile to the Jews, since he falls in love with a Jewish girl, the daughter of a much-hated usured. This fact tells us that some Christians at least are prepared to love Jews who have gentle manners and are willing to convert. Finally, Lorenzo and Jessica together create a world of love and harmony (symbolizing the harmony that will prevail when all Jews convert) that contrasts sharply with the harsh and hate-filled world of Shylock. We see the young lovers touched by the magic of a moonlit night but we see Shylock in the stark light of day. Jessica and Lorenzo are sensitive to the beauty of nature and of music; Shylock is a man who is damned because he has no music in his soul. In contrast with the idyllic young lovers, Shylock stands forth as an evil old miser.

SUBJECT BIBLIOGRAPHY AND GUIDE TO RESEARCH PAPERS

Life and Times of Shakespeare

Chute, Marchette, *Shakespeare of London,* New York, 1956. An excellent biography.

Halliday, F. E., *Shakespeare: A Pictorial Biography,* New York, 1956. Very good pictures.

Fluchère, Henri, *Shakespeare and the Elizabethans,* New York, 1956. Relates Shakespeare to the other dramatists of his time and to the world in which they lived.

Spencer, Theodore, *Shakespeare and the Nature of Man,* 1951. A discussion of the philosophical background of Shakespeare's England, with particular emphasis on man's place in nature.

Trevelyan, G. M., *History of England, Volume II: The Tudors and the Stuart Era,* New York, 1953. A good account of the history of Tudor England.

Tillyard, E. M. W., *The Elizabethan World Picture,* New York, 1944. An excellent description of the attitudes and manners in Shakespearean England, supplying important background material for the understanding of Shakespeare's work.

Shakespearean Theater Production

Adams, John Cranford, *The Globe Playhouse: Its Design and Equipment,* New York, 1942.

DeBanke, Cecile, *Shakespearean Production, Then and Now. A Manual for the Scholar Player,* New York, 1953.

Hodges, C. Walter, *The Globe Restored,* New York, 1954.

These books describe the way in which Shakespeare's plays were originally produced, and DeBanke's account includes helpful suggestions for the modern producer.

Historical and Literary Background for The Merchant of Venice

Cardozo, Dr. J. L., *The Contemporary Jew in the Elizabethan Drama,* Amsterdam, 1925. Shows that Jews were not present in Elizabethan England.

Divine, Thomas F., *Interest: an Historical and Analytical Study in Economics and Modern Ethics*, Milwaukee, 1959.

Lelyveld, Toby, *Shylock on the Stage*, Cleveland, 1960. Describes the different conceptions of Shylock held by the great actors in history in relation to the social attitudes of their times.

Muir, Kenneth, *Shakespeare's Sources*, London, 1957.

Nelson, B. N., *The Idea of Usury*, Princeton, 1949. A full history of usury throughout history.

Roth, Cecil, *A History of the Jews in England*, New York, 1949.

General Shakespearean Criticism

Charlton, H. B., *Shakespearean Comedy*, New York, 1938. Useful for a comparison of *The Merchant of Venice* with other Shakespearean comedies.

Coe, Charles Norton, *Shakespeare's* Villains, New York, 1957. Short essay on Shylock who is "overcharacterized."

Moulton, Richard G., *Shakespeare as a Dramatic Artist*, New York, 1929. Explanation of the way Shakespeare constructed his plays.

Spurgeon, Caroline T. E., *Shakespeare's Imagery and What it Tells Us*, New York, 1935.

Stoll, E. E., *Shakespeare Studies*, New York, 1942. Sees Shylock as an anti-Semitic, comic portrait.

Thorndike, Ashley, *English Comedy*, New York, 1929. Shows the relation between Shakespeare's comedies and other plays.

Criticism of The Merchant of Venice

Brown, John Russel, *Shakespeare and His Comedies*, London, 1957. An excellent short essay of *The Merchant of Venice.*

Granville-Barker, Harley, *Prefaces to Shakespeare*, Princeton, 1946. Criticism is incorporated into an essay on the staging of the play.

Hazlitt, William, *Characters of Shakespeare's Plays*, London, 1870. A romantic approach to *The Merchant of Venice*, extremely sympathetic to Shylock.

Jameson, Mrs. Anna, *Shakespeare's Heroines*, London, 1833. An excellent essay on Portia.

Palmer, John, *Comic Characters of Shakespeare*, London, 1946. Interesting remarks on Shylock as a comic character.

Van Doren, Mark, *Shakespeare*, New York, 1953. A modern essay emphasizing the use of language in *The Merchant of Venice* to create two distinct worlds: Venice and Belmont.

Wilson, J. D., *The Essential Shakespeare*, Cambridge, 1932. Touches on many different aspects of the play.

NOTES

NOTES

NOTES

NOTES

NOTES

NOTES

NOTES

NOTES

NOTES

NOTES

NOTES